Robert Samuel Wright, Henry Hobhouse

An Outline of Local Government and Local Taxation

in England and Wales, excluding the metropolis - together with some

considerations for amendment

Robert Samuel Wright, Henry Hobhouse

An Outline of Local Government and Local Taxation
in England and Wales, excluding the metropolis - together with some considerations for amendment

ISBN/EAN: 9783337287115

Printed in Europe, USA, Canada, Australia, Japan

Cover: Foto ©Suzi / pixelio.de

More available books at **www.hansebooks.com**

AN OUTLINE

OF

LOCAL GOVERNMENT AND LOCAL TAXATION

IN

ENGLAND AND WALES.

1884.

AN OUTLINE

of

LOCAL GOVERNMENT AND LOCAL TAXATION

in

ENGLAND AND WALES

(EXCLUDING THE METROPOLIS)

TOGETHER WITH

SOME CONSIDERATIONS FOR AMENDMENT.

BY

R. S. WRIGHT,
OF THE INNER TEMPLE,

AND

HENRY HOBHOUSE,
OF LINCOLN'S INN,

BARRISTERS-AT-LAW.

LONDON:

W. MAXWELL & SON, 8, BELL YARD, TEMPLE BAR,
Law Publishers and Booksellers.

P. S. KING & SON, Parliamentary Agency,
CANADA BUILDING, KING STREET, WESTMINSTER.

1884.

INTRODUCTION.

1. THE Government having announced in the Queen's Speech, that they have in preparation measures for the reform and improvement of Local Government and Taxation, it becomes of great importance that accurate information on these intricate subjects should be diffused as widely as possible.

It is hoped that the present work (which is founded on two memoranda privately circulated by us among members of Parliament in the year 1877) may be of use as an outline of Local Government as it at present exists, and as an index of the various areas, bodies and purposes which will have to be considered in any Scheme which may be adopted.

It also contains references to the Statutes and original authorities on the subject, which should make it useful to any student of Local Government and Taxation.

The original memoranda of 1877 were drawn from more than 500 public general Acts of Parliament, from decisions of Courts of Law, and various Blue Books,* and were revised by gentlemen of great local experience in different parts of

---

* A list of the most important of these Blue Books, and of the recent debates on Local Government, will be found at p. 117 below.

the country. They have now been further revised, amplified, and brought down to date in the present work.

2. We think that it must be apparent that the existing local organization is in many of its parts complicated and unequal to present requirements. The increase in population and in the requirements of the time has outgrown the capacity of local machinery created for more limited objects. The greatly increased duties thrown upon local bodies, and their powers to tax and incur debt, make it necessary that the local organization should be simplified and strengthened. In particular, the amount of local indebtedness has during the past ten or fifteen years assumed alarming proportions; it is annually growing at a rate which is out of proportion to the rate of growth of the property on which it is imposed; and, if much longer continued, it may result in an oppressive burden.

3. The main cause of the defectiveness of the existing organization seems to be the complication of the areas into which the country is subdivided for the different purposes of administration. This complication operates injuriously in two ways.

In the *first* place, it involves the concurrent existence of a number of distinct governing bodies independent of each other and conflicting sometimes in interest or policy, even when having to some extent the same area of jurisdiction. If one simple unit of local government were adopted for all purposes, there would be a single governing body, elected at one time and in one manner, and by one constituency; and this body, by itself or by its committees, would manage all the affairs of the locality on consistent principles; its proceedings would be subject to effective control by the ratepayers; and last, though not least, it would have one budget of expenditure and debt of the whole locality. At present the affairs of a country parish are for some purposes administered by overseers, appointed in one way. For other purposes it is part of a union, the affairs of which are administered by guardians, elected or appointed in another way. For other purposes it may have its school board, elected in a different way from the guardians. For other purposes it may be part of a highway district, differing in limits from the parish, union, or school district, and administered by a fourth distinct body. For other purposes, again, such as cemeteries or drainage, it may be apportioned among other distinct areas, with different governing bodies; while as regards police, licensing, asylums and other county affairs, it is governed by the justices. Under such circumstances, the man most anxious and competent to serve his locality with effect cannot do so. He has, in truth, no one locality. He is in different districts, with different populations, for different purposes.

In the *second* place, the same cause prevents the ratepayer from seeing or controlling the total of the indebtedness by which he may be affected. Parliament may see the growth of the local indebtedness of the country as a whole, but they cannot control it. The ratepayer alone could control its growth as it proceeds, but he cannot see it. The various debts which affect him—for county and borough buildings, for workhouses, for sanitary purposes, for cemeteries, for schools, for highways, &c., &c.—are contracted by different authorities for areas which are not conterminous. Even if it were possible to ascertain the aggregate of the amounts which affect himself, he does not in fact know it; for there is no one to state it to him. Nor, if he did know it, could he do anything effectual to control it. He cannot all at once bring pressure to bear upon the various governing bodies of the various districts in which he lives. If, on the other hand, his district were the same for all purposes and governed by one body, he would know its total debt in good time. He would jealously watch its growth. He would know the reason for every increase. In this way alone can economy be expected. The evil of growing indebtedness must be dealt with locally; but it cannot be dealt with locally until its existence and its probable results have been brought home to the ratepayer; and they cannot be brought home to the ratepayer without a simplification of areas and of governing bodies. This seems to be the first condition of improvement.

4. It is not unimportant to observe that the defectiveness of the existing local organization at once overwhelms the Local Government Board with details which ought to be locally settled, and makes its interposition less effectual. "As the local authorities are strengthened and the impediments to their good working removed, the necessity for interference by the central authority will be diminished, at the same time that the use and value of its supervision and of the information which it could communicate will be greatly increased. The existing confusion of things at once creates a necessity for perpetual interference, and makes the interference ineffectual."

5. It is now generally admitted that the whole subject of Local Government and Taxation ought to be considered with a view to certain lines being laid down for dealing with it systematically. No doubt any general measures will involve some disturbance of existing burdens and some interference

with individual interests; but there is as little doubt that the necessary disturbance of burdens will become greater and more difficult the longer improvement is postponed, or that the benefits to be expected will be sufficiently important and permanent to justify liberality in dealing with interests which may be affected.

SAM. WHITBREAD, M.P.
WM. RATHBONE, M.P.

7th April, 1884.

PREFACE.

The following work is based on two memoranda on Local Government written by Mr. Wright in the year 1877, which were privately circulated among members of Parliament and others interested in the subject. These memoranda have now been revised, amalgamated, brought down to date, and to some extent rearranged by Mr. Hobhouse, who alone is responsible for the accuracy of the present work. Chapters on Poor Law administration, and Licensing, and notes on various minor matters have been added.

The Tables of Local Taxation at pp. 79—92 have been carefully prepared by a gentleman familiar with such statistics, and are (it is hoped) as accurate as the nature of the returns will permit.

R. S. WRIGHT,
1, Paper Buildings, Temple.

H. HOBHOUSE,
2, Mitre Court Buildings, Temple.

10th April, 1884.

CONTENTS.

PART I.

GENERAL VIEW OF THE EXISTING ORGANIZATION OF LOCAL GOVERNMENT IN ENGLAND.

A.—*Existing Units of Local Government.*

	PAGE
CHAPTER I.	
THE PARISH	1
CHAPTER II.	
THE UNION	8
CHAPTER III.	
THE COUNTY	12
CHAPTER IV.	
THE BOROUGH	17
CHAPTER V.	
URBAN DISTRICTS	21

B.—*Matters which are Locally Administered.*

CHAPTER VI.	
POOR LAW ADMINISTRATION	24
CHAPTER VII.	
SANITARY PURPOSES	29
CHAPTER VIII.	
HIGHWAYS	34

CONTENTS.

CHAPTER IX.
Police 42

CHAPTER X.
Licensing 47

CHAPTER XI.
Lunatics 50

CHAPTER XII.
Schools 53

CHAPTER XIII.
Burial 56

CHAPTER XIV.
Drainage and Embankment 61

CHAPTER XV.
Valuation and Local Accounts 64

CHAPTER XVI.
Local Loans 69

PART II.

AMOUNT OF LOCAL TAXATION AND INDEBTEDNESS.

A.—General Remarks 73

B.—Tables of Local Taxation 79

PART III.

CONSIDERATIONS WITH A VIEW TO AMENDMENT OF LOCAL GOVERNMENT.

		PAGE
A.—AREAS	. . . .	93
B.—LOCAL AUTHORITIES	. . . .	100
C.—LOCAL TAXATION	. . . .	102

APPENDIX.

SPECIAL MATTERS.

I.—BRIDGES	106
II.—PRISONS	106
III.—WEIGHTS AND MEASURES, ETC.	107
IV.—CONTAGIOUS DISEASES (ANIMALS)	108
V.—REGISTRATION OF BIRTHS AND DEATHS . . .	108
VI.—VACCINATION	109
VII.—PUBLIC BATHS AND WASHHOUSES . .	109
VIII.—PUBLIC LIBRARIES AND MUSEUMS . . .	109
IX.—LIGHTING	110
X.—TRAMWAYS	111
XI.—ARTISANS AND LABOURERS' DWELLINGS . . .	111
XII.—FACTORIES AND WORKSHOPS	113
XIII.—MISCELLANEOUS SANITARY POWERS . . .	114
XIV.—FISHERY DISTRICTS	114
XV.—MARINE AND HARBOUR BOARDS . . .	115
XVI.—TAX COMMISSIONERS	115

INDEX OF PARLIAMENTARY PAPERS AND DEBATES . .	117
INDEX OF SESSIONS	118
GENERAL INDEX	119

NOTE TO PART I.

The scheme of this Part is as follows : Division A. deals with the different areas now forming the principal units of local administration. Of these the parish, county, and borough are ancient, the union and urban sanitary district of modern origin. The rural sanitary district (being usually co-extensive with the union) is not considered separately here.

Division B. deals with the principal matters which are locally administered. This is in the main a cross division, as the administration of each class of matters affects more than one class of areas. Thus "Poor Law purposes" affect the parish as well as the union, "Sanitary purposes" the rural as well as the urban districts, while the administration of "Highways" concerns the county and parish as well as the highway district. Again, "Burial" and "Schools" are administered in boroughs and parishes, and "Police" "Licensing" and "Lunatics" in county and borough areas. "Drainage" usually involves the creation of a new class of special areas. The last two chapters deal with matters of local finance.

Special matters of minor importance, or which could not conveniently be classed under the above heads, are dealt with in the Appendix (p. 105).

EXPLANATORY NOTE TO MARGINAL REFERENCES.

The numerous Statutes referred to in the marginal notes to the following Chapters are (to save space) quoted by their year only. The Session corresponding to each year will be found in the Index at p. 118. Where no chapter is given in the marginal note, the reference is to the last cited Act of the year named.

LOCAL GOVERNMENT.

[NOTE.—*Throughout this Memorandum the Metropolis must be understood to be excluded unless it is expressly mentioned.*]

PART I.

GENERAL VIEW OF THE EXISTING ORGANIZATION OF LOCAL GOVERNMENT IN ENGLAND.

A. *Existing Units of Local Government.*

CHAPTER I.

THE PARISH.

(1) Area of "*Parish.*"
(2) *Organization.*
(3) *Purposes and Expenses of Parish Organization.*

"PARISH," for most of the purposes of local government, now means the parish as defined for poor-law purposes, that is to say, a place for which a separate poor-rate is or can be made, or for which a separate overseer is or can be appointed. The parish in this sense is often only a part of the ancient civil parish, especially in the northern counties, in which separate overseers were in many cases appointed for each of the several townships included in the extensive parishes common in those counties (*a*) (*b*). It differs also in many cases from the ecclesiastical parish, principally through the operation of the Church Building and New Parishes Acts, under which particular districts have been formed into parishes for ecclesiastical purposes. (*c*)

(1) AREA.
1866, c. 113, s. 18.

Every part of England, including the bed of tidal rivers and the sea-shore to low water-mark, is now comprised in some poor-law parish. The number of such parishes is about 15,000, out of which about 5,000 are townships or other fractions of ancient civil parishes. (*d*)

1868, c. 122, s. 27.

Parishes are very unequal in extent and population. The average population is about 1,700, but a very large number have a population of less than 50. The greater number have a population between 300 and 1,000. No powers exist for the consolidation of small parishes; and no powers exist for the division of large parishes, except by Provisional Order made on the application of one-tenth in value of the owners and ratepayers—a proportion which has been obtained only in two or three instances. Isolated or detached portions of parishes may however be merged or constituted separate parishes by order of the Local Government Board without such application.

The boundaries of parishes never cut the boundaries of unions, which are merely aggregations of parishes; and there are only eighty-five parishes which extend into more counties than one; but parishes are frequently cut by the boundaries of boroughs and of local board districts. (e)

(2) ORGANIZATION.
i. Common vestry.
1818, c. 69.
1819, c. 12, s. 22.
1819, c. 85.
1850, c. 57.
1853, c. 65.

The ordinary organization of a parish for civil purposes consists of an assembly called a vestry, and of certain officers. Vestries are either common or select. Common vestries are meetings of all the rated inhabitants, who have one vote if rated at less than £50, and additional or plural votes (not exceeding a total of six) for every £25 above £50. (f) The rector or other incumbent, if present, is the chairman. In his absence a chairman is elected by the meeting. The chairman has an additional or casting vote.

ii. Select vestry.
1831, c. 60.

Select vestries are usually bodies elected by the rated householders in parishes with not less than 800 such householders under Hobhouse's Act (1831). This Act may be adopted by a two-thirds vote consisting of a majority of all the ratepayers who have been rated for a year. The consequence of adopting the Act is that, instead of a common vestry, a select vestry must be annually elected. The number of select vestrymen is to be twelve for every 1,000 rated householders, but not exceeding 120. The rector, or other incumbent, and churchwardens are ex officio members. The elected vestrymen retire by thirds annually. They must be resident householders rated at £10, or if the number of resident householders exceeds 3,000, at £40. The election, if a poll is demanded, must be by ballot. Each ratepayer has one vote. The Act also provides for the election of auditors, and for the publication of accounts of charities.

There are also select vestries in certain parishes appointed under local usages, and not under any Act. There are also select vestries regulated by local Acts.

The principal civil officers of the parish are the "overseers of the poor," who are appointed annually, within fourteen days from 25th of March, by the justices. The Poor Law Act of Elizabeth, 1601, directs that their number shall be from two to four, and that the churchwardens shall be associated as overseers with the nominated persons; but by later Acts provision is made for appointment of a single overseer in small places, and where there are no separate churchwardens for the poor-law parish the nominated overseers act alone. They ought to be good and substantial householders. Service of the office is compulsory, subject to appeal and to various exemptions and disqualifications. A woman is capable of being overseer. Where there is no fit inhabitant in a parish the justices may appoint an inhabitant householder of an adjoining parish, with his consent, and with a salary. The overseers have other duties besides those connected with the relief of the poor, *e.g.*, making out lists of jurors, and of parliamentary voters and burgesses.

iii. Parish officers. Overseers.
1601, c. 2.
1743, c. 38, s. 15.
1814, c. 91.
1819, c. 12.
1849, c. 8.
1852, c. 38.
1857, c. 19.
1866, c. 113.

A vestry may elect one or more salaried assistant overseers to perform all or any of the duties of overseers, and the persons so elected are appointed by the justices. The same person cannot be overseer and assistant. There is no general power for parishes to appoint collectors of rates. But under the Act of 1844 they may, by order of the Local Government Board, be appointed by the guardians of a "union" for any parish or parishes in the union. Where the guardians have appointed a collector, the vestry cannot elect an assistant overseer.

Assistant overseers, &c.
1819, c. 12, s. 7.
1844, c. 101, ss. 61, 62.
1866, c. 113.

In a parish with more than 2,000 population a permanent salaried vestry clerk may be elected by the vestry under an order obtained from the Local Government Board. His duty is ordinarily to perform or assist in the performance of the various functions of the churchwardens and overseers. The overseers are not exempt from any responsibility by reason of the appointment of a vestry clerk, assistant overseer, or collector. The Local Government Board have also a general power to remove paid parish officers employed in relation to poor relief.

Vestry clerk.
1850, c. 57.

1834, s. 48.

The rector, or other incumbent, besides being the regular chairman of the parish vestry, has also civil duties for purposes of registration of marriages and burials. He or a churchwarden or overseer may summon a vestry meeting. The parish clerk and sexton have no civil duties. In some parishes there still remain certain ancient manorial offices, such as the haywarden (i. e., guardian of fences) and pound-keeper. With respect to surveyors of highways and waywardens and parish constables, see Chs. VIII., IX.

Other officers.

1837, c. 45.

(4) PURPOSES AND EXPENSES OF PARISH ORGANIZATION.

The purposes of parish organization have been much diminished in number and importance by the Poor Law Amendment, Highway District, and Public Health Acts, which have made the union, highway, and sanitary districts the customary units for local government purposes.

1833, c. 90.

But in a considerable number of rural parishes the roads are still managed by parochial surveyors; in some large parishes a semi-urban organization exists for lighting and similar purposes under the Lighting and Watching Act (1833); in a great number of parishes (not being within municipal boroughs) the Elementary Education Acts are administered by parochial school boards, and burial grounds are maintained by parochial burial boards; and some few parishes have a special organization under local acts. With these exceptions and a few more (*g*), there are now hardly any matters which are parochially administered, and the parish may for the present purpose be regarded mainly as the constituent unit of all unions and as a district for the collection of rates and for the preparation of jury lists and the registers of parliamentary and municipal voters.

Poor rate.
1601, c. 2.

The parish rate is the poor-rate, which is levied by the overseers. It is assessed and levied by a uniform and equal poundage on the value of the lands and houses in the parish as shown in the Valuation List of the union in which the parish is comprised. (See Chs. VI., XV.) There are very few expenses which the vestry or the overseers can by their own authority charge on the poor-rate. The demands upon it are for the most part made by special authorities, such as the school board; or by external authorities, such as the union or the county (*h*).

Parish property.
1814, c. 137.
1819, c. 12.
1835, c. 69.
1842, c. 18.
1850, c. 57.
1860, c. 30.
1861, c. 125.
1876, c. 62.
Inclosure Acts.
1845, c. 118, ss. 10, 73.
1876, c. 58, s. 25.

Buildings, lands, and other property belonging to a parish are ordinarily vested in the churchwardens and overseers (who are incorporated for this purpose by the Act of 1819), and may be let by them. Under the Inclosure Acts (1845 & 1876) village greens and public recreation grounds are vested in these officers. Under the Acts of 1835 & 1842, the guardians of the parish or of the union including the parish may, with the approval of the Local Government Board and the consent of a majority of ratepayers and owners, sell, purchase, and dispose of workhouses, lands, and other parish property. The Acts of 1850 & 1861, enable vestry rooms and overseers' offices to be provided in populous parishes.

NOTES.

Note (a). The following note shows the historical relations of the different parochial areas :— *Township and Parish.*

(i.) The most ancient unit is the township (or tything or vill) which was organized for the maintenance of the peace under an elected tythingman, headborough, or borsholder, and to which there was often attached as a lesser member a hamlet or other dependency. Lord Coke estimates the number of townships at 8,803. (1 Inst. 116a.)

(ii.) On the township was superimposed the ecclesiastical parish, which sometimes corresponded with the township, sometimes (especially in the south) included only a part of a township, sometimes (especially in the north) included two or more and often many townships, and sometimes had no relation to the township area. It is not known how or when the division of the county into ecclesiastical parishes was made, but it appears to have been nearly complete in the time of Edward the First. (Taxatio Ecclésiastica, 1288—1292, which however is, strictly speaking, a list of taxable benefices, not parishes.) The area of the parish seems to have been determined partly by manors, partly by the lands which paid tithe to the church. Places which for any reason were exempt from tithe were generally also extra-parochial.

(iii.) During the 13th and 14th centuries the parish remained chiefly an ecclesiastical area and the vestry an ecclesiastical assembly. Meanwhile, the civil matters of the locality were usually administered in, and the constables, haywards, and other civil officers appointed by, the manor court, which had in most places replaced the old township organization. From about the year 1535 (when the parish churchwardens became charged by statute with the civil duty of poor relief) the parish may be regarded as a civil unit. This "ancient civil parish" (so called here for distinction from the modern civil or poor law parish) coincides in general with the ecclesiastical parish, subject to accidental or customary exceptions. See *R. v. Watson*, L. R., 3 Q. B. 762, for an instance of a place titheable in one parish, but rateable in another.

(iv.) The modern civil or poor-law parish, in so far as it adopts the township (see next note), is a revival of the more ancient unit. For the "highway parish," see Ch. VIII. note (a).

Note (b). The poor-law parish differs from the ancient civil parish in many cases, partly through usages by which townships or other sub-divisions of ancient parishes have acquired a right of appointing separate overseers or of being separately rated for the poor, and partly by the operation of the following statutes :— *Poor-law parish.*

1662.—C. 12, recites the largeness of the parishes in the northern and other counties, and enacts that in every "township or village" within such counties there shall be separate overseers.

1819.—C. 95. Where a parish partly within and partly without a town corporate or liberty had for sixty years before 1819 been customarily divided for poor-law purposes, the separation is confirmed.

1857.—C. 19, s. 1. Places being, or reputed to be, extra-parochial, and entered separately in the census of 1851, and not rated or contributing in 1857 for the relief of the poor, are made parishes " for all the purposes of the assess-"ment to the poor-rate, the relief of the poor, the county, police, or "borough rate, the burial of the dead, the removal of nuisances, the regis-"tration of parliamentary and municipal voters, and the registration of "births and deaths;" and in any place being, or reputed to be, extra-parochial, and not being rated or contributing for the poor, overseers may be appointed. By s. 4, the Quarter Sessions of a county or the Recorder in a borough may, on the application of the owners and occupiers of two-thirds in value of the land in an extra-parochial place, annex it to any parish with the consent of that parish. (And see s. 78.)

1867.—Under c. 106 (the Poor Law Amendment Act, 1867), s. 3, detached parts of a parish may be merged in the surrounding parish, or a large parish may be divided by Provisional Order of the Local Government Board, made after public local inquiry, and on an application made by "one-tenth part in value "of owners of property and of ratepayers in the parish or parishes respec-"tively interested in the subject."

1868.—C. 122 (the Poor Law Amendment Act, 1868), s. 27, provided that every place being or reputed to be extra-parochial, and which was not on the 25th December, 1868, organized as or annexed to a poor-law parish, should be for all civil purposes incorporated with the adjoining parish having the longest common boundary; and also that every riparian parish should extend to low-water mark or mid-stream.

<small>1876, c. 61.
1879, o. 54.
1882, c. 58.</small>

1876.—The Divided Parishes Acts now provide for the merger of detached parts of parishes, or for their organization as separate parishes.

<small>1844, c. 101, s. 22.</small>

But by the Poor Law Amendment Act, 1844, the creation of new poor-law parishes by the appointment of separate overseers is now prohibited except in the cases provided for by the subsequent Acts above mentioned.

<small>*Ecclesiastical parish.*</small>

<small>1856, c. 104, s. 25.</small>

Note (c). The Church Building Acts, 1818 to 1855, contain numerous and complicated provisions for enabling the Church Building Commissioners to divide parishes for ecclesiastical purposes. In 1856, these commissioners ceased to exist, their powers being transferred to the Ecclesiastical Commissioners. As this body have now, under the new Parishes Acts, 1843 to 1869, full power with certain consents to divide any parish into two or more separate parishes "for any ecclesiastical purposes whatsoever," the Church Building Acts are become to a great extent obsolete. Where a new ecclesiastical parish is formed under these Acts, separate churchwardens are elected; but these have no poor law or civil functions, and the inhabitants of the new parish retain their right to vote for the churchwardens of the old parish (*R.* v. *Stephens*, 32 L. J. Q. B. 90). By the census of 1881, it appears that there are 6,598 ecclesiastical parishes (consisting of 9107 constituent parts) which are not conterminous with civil or poor law parishes. The total number of ecclesiastical parishes seems, roughly estimated, to be about 13,000.

<small>*Number, &c.*</small>

Note (d). The 5000 poor-law parishes, which are townships or other parts of ancient civil, or ecclesiastical parishes, are chiefly in Yorkshire, Northumberland, Lancashire, Cheshire and Durham. In 1878, there were 788 poor-law parishes, containing less than 50, and 6000 containing less than 300 inhabitants.

THE PARISH.

Note (*e*). In 1880, there were 726 parishes, partly within and partly without urban sanitary districts. These cut the boundaries of 227 boroughs, 688 local government, and 49 improvement Act districts. (See Parliamentary Papers, ᵾᵾᵾ.) — *Boundaries.*

Note (*f*). In a common vestry, persons jointly rated may have votes according to their respective shares, but if only one of them attends he may vote as if the whole were his own. Officers of rated corporations may vote on behalf of their corporations. Non-payment of rates three months due disqualifies for voting. Owners compounding under the Act of 1819, may vote as ratepayers. — *Common Vestry.* 1819, c.12, s.22.

Note (*g*). The following Acts may still be adopted in any *rural* parish (*i.e.* one not included in an urban sanitary district), the Lighting and Watching Act, the Baths and Washhouses Acts, and the Public Libraries and Museums Acts. (See Appendix, pp. 109, 110.) The vestry of any parish whether urban or rural, (if not in a municipal borough) may appoint a burial board. (See Chapter XIII.) — *Parish Acts.*

Under an Act of 1860, (now practically superseded in urban districts by s. 164 of the Public Health Act, 1875), the vestry of any poor-law parish with a population exceeding 500, may by a majority of two-thirds resolve to purchase lease, or accept grants of land for forming or improving any public walk, exercise, or playground. Commissioners may be appointed for the execution of the Act, and when half the cost of the improvement has been voluntarily subscribed, may levy an improvement rate not exceeding 6*d*. in the pound. — 1860, c. 30.

Under the Poor Law Amendment Act, 1867, the vestry of a rural parish may provide and maintain a fire-engine and its accoutrements for public use at the cost of the poor-rate. — 1867, c. 106, s. 29.

Note (*h*). The Poor Law Act of Elizabeth empowers the justices to rate any parish in a county in aid of another parish in the same county which cannot maintain its own poor. But this provision appears to be wholly obsolete. — *Rates.* 1601, c. 2.

See, as to church-rates, the Compulsory Church-rate Abolition Act, 1868, which abolished compulsory levy of church-rates, with a saving where there are mortgages of the rate, &c. The Act authorizes the appointment of a body of "church trustees" to receive, hold and administer property for ecclesiastical purposes. For rates leviable in parishes for highways and for other special purposes, see Chapters on "Highways," &c., below. — 1868, c. 109.

CHAPTER II.

THE UNION.

(1) *Area of Unions.*
(2) *Organization.*
(3) *Purposes and Expenses of Union Organization.*

<small>(1) AREA.
1834, c. 76.
1844, c. 101.
1867, c. 106.
1868, c. 122.
1876, c. 61.
1879, c. 54.
1882, c. 58.</small>

THE present union organization has been created under the Poor Law Amendment Act, 1834, which established a poor law commission with extensive powers of organization and control. Their assistant-commissioners made a progress through the whole country, and grouped the parishes as appeared most convenient. The general idea on which the union was formed was that of taking a market town as a centre, and uniting the surrounding parishes, the inhabitants of which resorted to its market, such a centre being supposed to be convenient for the attendance of guardians and of parish officers. A limiting principle was, that in the first instance the union should be small enough for the guardians to have a personal knowledge of all the details of its management; and it seems to have been intended that, as the business became simplified and understood, the area might be enlarged. The situations of existing workhouses determined the limits of some unions. Various other local circumstances and feelings must have been allowed to modify the general plan. Unions under the former Acts were respected, and have only gradually disappeared (*a*). Extra-parochial places could not be included in unions until later legislation had made them parochial, but are all now so included. Many single parishes have been constituted "unions" under separate boards of guardians. The result has been that the areas of unions are unequal in size, and often irregular in form, nor do they respect municipal, urban sanitary or county boundaries, the only boundary which they never cut being that of the poor-law parish (*b*).

<small>*Alteration, &c. of Unions.*
1834, s. 32.
1844, s. 38.
1868, s. 4.
1876, s. 11.
1879, c. 54, s. 8.</small>

Under the Poor Law Amendment Acts, 1834 to 1876, the Local Government Board have power to dissolve any existing union and to add or take away parishes, and to constitute any severed parish or parishes a separate "union." The same authority may also, under the Act of 1879, with the consent of the guardians combine any two or more unions for any poor-law purposes, and invest a joint committee with any of the powers of guardians over the combined area. Unions and parishes may be combined into districts for pauper schools and asylums for the houseless poor. (As to school districts, see Ch. XII., p. 54. There are no asylum districts outside the metropolitan area). The Act of 1834 also contains provisions enabling a complete consoli- 1834, ss. 33-36 dation of all the parishes in a union to be made for all purposes of poor relief, settlement and rating, but these seem to be now almost obsolete.

The administrative authority in a "union" is the board of (2) ORGANIZA-
guardians. This board consists of guardians annually elected in April *Guardians.*
by the constituent parishes and of the county justices resident in the 1834.
union as ex officio members. The number of guardians to be elected 1867.
by each parish is fixed by the Local Government Board, who have 1868, s. 6.
power to group small parishes for this purpose, subject to the rule that every parish of more than 300 population must have at least one guardian assigned to it. One effect of this rule is, that the representation is often extremely disproportionate to population. The Local Government Board may also (under the Acts of 1876 and 1882) divide any parish into wards for the election of guardians and alter the wards, and may (under the Act of 1834), with the consent of the majority of the owners and ratepayers of a union, extend the guardians' term of office to three years (c). Where there is a failure in any parish to elect guardians, the former guardians may continue to serve for another year.

The qualification for an elected guardian is fixed by the Local Government Board, but must not exceed £40 rating. The voting is by papers, and the electors are the owners and ratepayers of the parish, with plural votes at the rate of one vote for every £50 rating (or part of £50) up to six votes. Owners must claim and be registered in order to be entitled to vote, and may vote by proxy, if non-resident. They may vote both as owners and also as occupiers, if qualified in both ways. Corporate bodies may vote by their officers.

The usual officers of a board of guardians are a clerk, a treasurer, *Officer.*
relieving officers, registrars of births and deaths (appointed by but not under the control of the guardians), one or more medical officers (or "parish doctors"), a vaccination officer, and the necessary officers in workhouses. There may be also a paid valuer and paid collectors of rates.

The board may form committees for relief in districts of their union. They must annually appoint an assessment committee for purposes of valuation.

Control.

The Local Government Board (as the successors of the former Poor Law Commissioners and Poor Law Board) have comprehensive powers of control over guardians. Firstly, they are empowered to issue general orders for regulating the election of guardians, the meetings and procedure of guardians, the mode and conditions of outdoor relief, the management of workhouses, the mode of obtaining contributions from parishes, the appointment, dismissal, payment and conduct of union officers, the accounts of the guardians and of their officers, and generally all matters relating to the execution of the poor-laws. Secondly, they issue special orders in particular cases under particular provisions of the Poor Law Acts or for enforcing performance of duties. Thirdly, they appoint district auditors, who are civil servants of the State, and who audit, under the control of the Local Government Board, the accounts of parish, as well as of union officers, and have power to disallow and surcharge illegal payments, subject to an appeal which, however, is not of much value, since the costs must be paid by the parish or union even if it succeeds, and they are settled by the auditor himself.

Audit.
1844, ss. 32–49.
1852, c. 81, s. 33.
1868, c. 109, s. 3.
1879, c. 6.

(3) PURPOSES OF UNION ORGANIZATION.

The purposes of the union organization are—(i.) the local administration of the poor-laws; (ii.) the preparation of the valuation lists on which the poor-rate is assessed; (iii.) in rural places the local administration of the sanitary laws; (iv.) registration of births and deaths; (v.) the enforcement of vaccination; and (vi.) and the enforcement of the Elementary Education Acts in places having no school boards and not being municipal boroughs. (See as to these purposes, Chs. VI., VII., XII., XV., and Appendix, pp. 108, 109.)

Rating.

The union has not (generally speaking) any direct rating powers. It collects its funds (and also the county rate) by means of orders upon the overseers of parishes. Nevertheless the union must be regarded as being in substance the rating authority in relation to the poor-rate, because it controls the valuation, enforces the collection, and, in rural places, determines by far the greater part of the expenditure which is defrayed out of that rate. There is now hardly any part of this expenditure which is not borne by the "common fund" of the union, which fund was instituted in 1884 for workhouse and establishment purposes, but on which there has since been thrown practically the whole cost of poor relief, valuation, registration, vaccination, and (in rural places) all general sanitary purposes (*d*).

See 1865, c. 79, ss. 1, 9.

NOTES.

Note (*a*). Before 1782 many unions of parishes had been constituted under special Acts, such as that for the Metropolitan counties (1662); those for Bristol and Gloucester in the reigns of William III. and Anne, and certain other incorporations of hundreds, towns, and districts. There were also combinations of small parishes for a common workhouse under an Act of 1723. In 1782, Gilbert's Act provided for the constitution of unions by agreement of parishes, with elected and nominated guardians. Unions under this Act were financially combined for the purposes of indoor relief only, and they did not form consolidated areas, but consisted merely of such parishes within a radius of ten miles from the workhouse as chose to unite. Nor was there any provision for central control. Nearly all these old unions and incorporations have now ceased to exist.

Old Unions.
1662, c. 12.
1796, c. 10.
1723, c. 7.
1782, c. 83.

Note (*b*). In 1883 there were 617 "unions" in England and Wales (besides 30 in the metropolis), containing 14,739 parishes, and a population of 22,154,000.

Of these "unions" 13 are incorporations or single parishes, in which poor relief is administered by governors or guardians or other authorities, constituted under local Acts. The rest are unions or parishes with boards of guardians under the Poor Law Amendment Acts.

These unions vary in size from West Derby (Lancashire), with a population of 360,000, down to Sedbergh (Yorkshire), with 4000, and Hoo (Kent), with 3100 inhabitants. About 580 unions are wholly or partly rural. The ordinary size of a purely rural union appears to be from 60 to 100 square miles, and its population is ordinarily from 12,000 to 20,000.

In 1882 there were 176 unions which included parts of two or more counties, 29 of these being each in three counties, and 4 others being each in four counties. Of the 617 unions, only 8 were co-extensive with municipal boroughs. Only two counties (Northumberland and Cumberland) have their boundaries coincident with those of unions.

Number, &c.

Note (*c*). In 1883 there were 24 unions (mostly populous) which had triennial elections of guardians. In 22 cases the whole board retires every third year, while in 2 cases one third retire each year.

Elections.

Note (*d*). For further details as to poor-law expenditure, see notes to Chapter VI.

Expenses.

CHAPTER III.

THE COUNTY.

(1) *Area of County.*
(2) *County Organization.*
(3) *Purposes and Expenses of County Organization.*

(1) AREA.

ENGLAND comprises forty counties properly so called, North and South Wales six each. Besides these, certain liberties (Ely, Peterborough, and Ripon), and eighteen boroughs, which are "counties of cities" or "counties of towns," are treated as separate counties for many purposes (*a*). Boroughs with separate Courts of Quarter Sessions are also for many purposes treated as distinct from counties (see Ch. IV., p. 19).

1828, c. 43.
1829, c. 46.
1836, c. 12.
1859 (2), c. 65.

Every county proper is divided into petty sessional divisions, each of which may consist of any number of parishes or parts of parishes. The distribution of divisions is made by the Quarter Sessions, and it cannot be altered for ten years where it has been made generally for the whole county, nor for twenty-one years where it has been made specially for a part of the county, except that, for the purpose of assimilating a division to a poor-law union, a division may be altered within three years from its constitution. An area cannot be made a petty sessional division unless five justices reside or usually act within it. These divisions are made for convenience in the administration of justice, and, perhaps, with a view of localising the magistracy. Any magistrate of the county is legally capable of acting in any division of the county, but it is a settled practice that, except in exceptional cases, a magistrate acts only in his own division. These divisions must be distinguished both from parliamentary divisions and from "ridings, parts or divisions of a county;" an expression which refers to the cases in which a county really consists of two or more counties with distinct commissions of the peace, *e.g.*, Yorkshire, Lincolnshire, or Sussex (*b*).

THE COUNTY.

The organization of an ordinary county consists of the following persons and bodies:— (2) ORGANIZATION.

- (1) A lord lieutenant appointed by commission. He represents the Crown for military purposes, and is nominally the commander of the county militia. He appoints deputy lieutenants and also recommends persons for the commission of the peace. 1832, c. 49, s. 29.
- (2) A custos rotulorum (keeper of the records) who is usually appointed by commission issued under the Royal sign manual. He is usually the same person as the lord lieutenant, and is the principal justice of the county. 1545, c. 1. 1688, c. 21.
- (3) A sheriff, formerly elected, but now annually selected by the Crown out of three persons (having lands in the county) nominated by the judges and privy councillors in the Exchequer Court, and appointed by warrant signed by the clerk of the Privy Council. The sheriff is the principal representative and agent of the Crown in the execution of the law, and, in that capacity, summons juries, tries compensation cases, and executes the writs of the superior courts. He is also the returning officer in county elections. He cannot during his term of office act as a justice. He must appoint an under-sheriff. 1340, st. 1, c. 7. 1559, st. 2, c. 8. 1662, c. 21.
- (4) A coroner or coroners (having lands in the county), usually elected by the freeholders of the county or district of the county (c).
- (5) Justices, qualified by an estate in possession of £100 a year or by one in reversion, &c. of £300 a year, or by two years' assessment to the inhabited house duty at £100, and appointed by a commission of the peace for the county. The duties of the county justices are partly judicial and partly administrative, and are exercised both in and out of (quarter) sessions. The Court of General or Quarter Sessions is held by all the justices of and for the county. A Petty Sessions consists of any two or more justices of the county acting in a petty sessional division. A Special Sessions is a Petty Sessions summoned for a special purpose by notice to all the justices of the petty sessional division. The justices in each petty sessional division have a clerk (d). 1743, c. 20. 1875, c. 54.

1879, c. 49, s. 20.
- (6) A clerk of the peace, appointed by the custos rotulorum as his deputy, but removable by the justices. 1545, c. 1. 1688, c. 21. 1864, c. 65.
- (7) A county treasurer, surveyor and other officers (e).

(3) PURPOSES OF COUNTY ORGANIZATION.

The purposes of the county organization are of two kinds, namely:—

a. Imperial purposes, the more important of which are the maintenance of the Queen's peace, the Militia, the local administration of justice, and parliamentary representation.

b. Local government purposes, the more important of which are the county bridges and main roads, shire-halls and other county buildings, police, asylums, licensing, the execution of the Contagious Diseases (Animals), the Weights and Measures, and other like Acts, and the control, by way of appeal or otherwise, under various Acts, of minor local authorities. (For these purposes see Chs. VIII.—XI. and Appendix, pp. 106—108.)

County Rate.
1852, c. 81.
1858, c. 33.
1866, c. 78.
1877, c. 66.

The ordinary expenditure of the county is defrayed principally out of a county rate, supplemented by contributions for certain purposes from the treasury and from independent boroughs (*f*). Abstracts of the accounts must be published, and must be sent to the Local Government Board, and to guardians of unions. The county rate is an assessment made by the county justices, not on individual properties, but on the several parishes in the county. A committee of Quarter Sessions ascertains the total of the net rateable value of each parish, and apportions the whole required amount accordingly, and precepts for the amount required from a parish are sent to the guardians of the union in which the parish is included. The guardians pay the amount to the county treasurer and recover it by order from the overseers of the parish. The overseers raise it in the parish by poor rates. The committee of justices are not bound by the poor-rate valuation. They may alter any such valuation for the purposes of the county rate, or they may make a new valuation, subject in either case to appeal to the whole Quarter Sessions.

NOTES.

Liberties.

1844, c. 61. And see c. 92, s. 8 (Coroners).
1842, c. 37 (taxes).
1858, c. 68 (police).
1850, c. 105.
1883, c. 18.

Note (*a*). There were formerly many detached parts of counties, and also many liberties independent of any county, and governed by their own justices, &c. But by an Act of 1844, all detached parts of counties were merged (with certain savings now practically gone) in the parliamentary counties to which they were assigned for parliamentary purposes by the Reform Act, 1832. And by an Act of 1850, provision was made for the merger of liberties by Order in Council on application of the authorities concerned. Under that Act and the Municipal Corporations Act, 1883, nearly all the liberties have now been merged, or are about to be merged in the adjoining counties, except Ely, Peterborough, Ripon, Cawood (in Yorkshire), and

Haverfordwest. Of these Ely has a chief bailiff, custos rotulorum, clerk of the peace, coroner, county rate, and quarter sessions. Ripon has all these except the first two, Haverfordwest has a lord-lieutenant, coroner, and court of quarter sessions, and Peterborough is a separate county for police and other purposes. All these liberties have separate commissions of the peace.

1836, c. 87.
1837, c. 53.
1856, c. 69, s. 30.
1882, c. 49,
s. 49, Sch. I.
c. 50, s. 248.

Note (*b*). The ancient division of counties into hundreds (lathes, wapentakes, &c.) is nearly obsolete, but the parliamentary divisions of counties are still founded upon it, and the hundred is still separately liable for damage by riot and in some cases for its own bridges and main roads. (See 1827, c. 31, 1878, c. 77, s. 20, and as to appointment of high constables for hundreds, 1869, c. 47.)

Hundreds, &c.

In 1881 there were 715 petty sessional divisions in England and Wales, and 830 hundreds.

There are 85 parishes, 182 unions and 14 municipal boroughs (Abingdon, Bristol, Burton, Oxford, Peterborough, Stalybridge, Stamford, Stockport, Sudbury, Tamworth, Thetford, Warrington, Yarmouth and Cardigan), and 21 urban sanitary districts which extend into more counties than one.

Note (*c*). The county coroner is an officer chosen in pursuance of the Queen's writ, by the freeholders of the county (without limit of value), and is paid by salary out of the county rate. He appoints a deputy and other officers, who are paid by fees. His duties are to hold inquiries in cases of sudden deaths, treasure trove, &c., and to act as the sheriff's deputy in executing certain writs (1276, 1844, s. 22).

Coroner.
1275, St. West.
1276, Off. Cor.
1340, St. 1, c. 8.
1354, c. 6.
1487, c. 2.
1751, c. 29.
1837, c. 68.

A large county is usually divided into districts, by Order in Council made on petition of quarter sessions, and a separate coroner is then elected for each district, and acts only within his district, but is coroner for the whole county (1844, s. 19).

1843, c. 12.
c. 83.
1844, c. 92.
1860, c. 116.

In many places, "franchise coroners" are appointed for manors, hundreds, parishes, &c., by lords of manors or other persons, and such coroners are often paid out of the county rate (1860, s. 8). Coroners for quarter sessions boroughs are ordinarily appointed by the council, and paid by fees.

1882, c. 50, s. 171.

Note (*d*). There are also some county justices ex officio or by Act of Parliament, *e. g.*, the Commissioners of Metropolitan police are justices for Berkshire and Buckinghamshire. The justices in a county are incorporated for the purposes of county loans. See the Local Loans Act, 1875. For other purposes, they are not a corporation, but under the County Property Acts, 1858 and 1871, all lands, &c., purchased or hired by the county justices are vested in the clerk of the peace and his successors.

Justices.
1875, c. 83, s. 36.
1858, c. 92.
1871, c. 14.

Note (*e*). Several counties have an exceptional organization.

Exceptions.

Yorkshire is for all practical purposes (except assizes, sheriff and coroner) three counties. Lincolnshire is three counties for some purposes, and four for others. Cambridgeshire, Essex, Suffolk and Sussex are each two counties for certain purposes. Cambridgeshire and Huntingdon have a common lord lieutenant. So have Cumberland and Westmoreland.

See as to General and Quarter Sessions in Lancashire the local Act, 1798, c. lviii.; as to Sussex, 1865, c. 37; Berwick-on-Tweed, 1836, c. 103, s. 6; Hertfordshire and St. Albans, 1874, c. 45.

County Rate. **Note** (*f*). The following are the principal purposes, the expenses of which are chargeable on the county rate :—

  i. County bridges and half the cost of maintaining main roads. (Ch. VIII., App. p. 106.)

1826, c. 63.
1837, c. 24.
  ii. Other county buildings, viz., shire-halls, court houses, judges' lodgings, police stations, justices' rooms and lock-ups.

  iii. Lunatic asylums, and the maintenance of pauper lunatics without settlement who are not irremovable. (Ch. XI.)

  iv. Maintaining and contributing to reformatory and industrial schools. (Ch. XII.)

1826, c. 64, s. 22.
  v. Prosecution and removal of prisoners.

  vi. Salaries of clerks of the peace, justices' clerks and county treasurer.

  vii. Allowances to high and special constables.

  viii. Coroners' salaries and expenses.

1825, c. 50.
1843, c. 18.
  ix. Clerk of peace's expenses in respect of registration of parliamentary voters and jury lists.

  x. Forming petty sessional divisions and polling districts.

1818, c. 75.
  xi. Removal of paupers without settlement, and burial of dead bodies cast on shore.

  xii. The local administration of the Acts relating to adulteration, contagious diseases (animals), petroleum, explosives, and weights and measures. (Ch. X., App. pp. 107, 108.)

The expenses of the police are payable out of a separate police rate, raised in a similar way to the county rate.

Several of the above classes of expenditure (*i.e.* police, criminal prosecutions, lunatics, and reformatory and industrial schools), though primarily chargeable on the county (or police) rate, are eventually defrayed in part by Treasury subventions out of Imperial taxation. For the contributions of Quarter Sessions boroughs towards county expenditure, see Ch. IV., p. 19.

CHAPTER IV.

THE BOROUGH.

(1) *Area of Borough.*
(2) *Organization.*
(3) *Purposes and Expenses of Borough Organization.*
(4) *Separate Commission of the Peace.*
(5) *Separate Court of Quarter Sessions.*

The only boroughs which are generally important for purposes of local government are "municipal boroughs," *i. e.*, boroughs governed under the Municipal Corporations Act, 1835, and amending Acts, all of which are now consolidated and repealed by the Act of 1882 (*a*). The boundaries of these boroughs have not been settled upon any general principle. They divide parishes and counties. They are divided by unions. They are often not conterminous with the parliamentary boroughs bearing the same name. In some cases they are not even conterminous with the urban sanitary district bearing the same name. They have, however, been generally adopted as units by the Sanitary Acts and by the Elementary Education Acts. They are usually divided into wards (*b*). (1) AREA. 1882, c. 50.

Boroughs are governed by corporations composed of a mayor, aldermen, and burgesses (or citizens), acting by a town council in which the burgesses are represented by from twelve to forty-eight town councillors. The burgesses or voters ordinarily consist of persons qualified by occupation of a building within the borough, and by residence within seven miles of it, and by rating to and payment of the poor and borough rates. There are also in many boroughs freemen or other customary burgesses. The burgesses elect councillors annually by ballot, and the council choose the aldermen and mayor. The qualification for a councillor is £1,000 property or £30 rating, if the borough is divided into four or more wards, or £500 property or £15 rating in undivided boroughs. But since 1880, any person qualified to vote in the election of councillors may be elected a councillor, though if he cease to reside in the borough he must have the property qualification. If the borough is divided into wards the councillors are apportioned (2) ORGANIZATION.

among and separately elected in the several wards. The mayor and aldermen are chosen from among the councillors or persons qualified to be councillors. The mayor holds office for one year, councillors for three years, aldermen for six years. The council appoint a town clerk and a treasurer, and other necessary officers. The council may appoint general or special committees of its own members for any purpose.

(3) PURPOSES OF BOROUGH ORGANIZATION.

The principal functions of the council are, under the Municipal Corporations Act, the lighting and watching of the borough; under the Public Health Act, the execution of the sanitary laws; and under the Elementary Education Act, 1876, the enforcement of that Act where there is no school board. They have power to make bye-laws for various purposes.

Expenses.
1882, ss. 144, 197.

Their expenses are ordinarily defrayed out of the borough fund, supplemented by a uniform borough-rate, leviable on the same basis as or out of the poor-rate. They may levy a watch rate over the whole borough, or specially over a part of it. Some boroughs have large corporate estates. But corporate lands cannot be sold, mortgaged, or (except for certain terms) leased without the consent of the Treasury or an Act of Parliament. Accounts must be annually sent to the Local Government Board, and laid before Parliament.

(4) SEPARATE COMMISSION.

1882, ss. 154, 158.

In every borough the mayor and last ex-mayor are justices of the peace for the borough for the time being. Moreover, a separate commission of the peace has been granted to many boroughs, and may be granted to any others. A separate commission does not of itself involve any exemption from the county-rate or from the jurisdiction of the county justices to act in the borough in petty sessions, or to act in matters concerning the borough at the county Quarter Sessions (*c*). It merely enables the borough justices under the commission to act in the borough as if they were county justices acting in and for a separate petty sessional division. But in practice, where there is a separate commission, the county justices do not ordinarily sit in the borough. Where there is a separate commission for a borough, a clerk to the borough justices is appointed. No qualification by estate is required in the case of justices for a borough. Every borough with a separate commission of the peace is a separate licensing division.

1882, s. 161.

A salaried police magistrate may be appointed in any municipal borough by the Secretary of State on the application of the council.

(5) SEPARATE QUARTER SESSIONS.

In addition to (or even without) a separate commission of the peace, the Crown may grant to a borough a separate court of Quarter Sessions, which involves a salaried recorder as judge of the court, a coroner and a clerk of the peace. The court is held not, as in a county, by the justices, but by the recorder as sole judge. When such a court has been granted, the borough becomes exempt by express enactment 1882, s. 150. from liability to be rated to the county-rate, and a borough-rate in the nature of a county-rate becomes leviable by the council. Nevertheless the borough continues liable to pay to the county the expenses of the prosecution, at the county assizes or Quarter Sessions, of prisoners from the borough, and of maintaining them from the time of commitment. And in the case of all boroughs which before 1832 were liable to contribute to county expenses, the borough continues liable also to pay to the county a proportion of the ordinary county expenditure other than that of coroners' inquests, county prisoners, main roads, expenses arising 1882, s. 152. under the Adulteration Acts, and Weights and Measures Act, and other than such expenditure as is specially provided for. (See Chapters IX., XI., for *Police, Lunatics,* &c.) Liverpool, for example, contributes about £11,000 yearly towards the general county expenditure (*d*) (*e*).

NOTES.

Note (*a*). There appear to be about 130 ancient boroughs, which are not under *Unreformed* the Municipal Corporations Act, 1882. Many of them are now small villages. Many *Corporations.* of them have justices of their own by charter or prescription, and some of their 1883, c. 18. charters contain a non-intromittant clause. Some of them still retain a separate licensing jurisdiction. The Municipal Corporations Act, 1883, provided that all these places with unreformed corporations should, in 1886, cease to be corporate boroughs, and (with certain savings) lose their franchises, unless before that time charters are granted by the Crown, applying the Municipal Corporations Acts to any of these places. The result of this will be that in 1886, all English boroughs (except London) will be under the same law.

Note (*b*). In 1883, there were 251 boroughs, divided into about 760 wards, *Number, &c.* having a population of about 8¼ millions, and an assessable value of nearly 35 millions. Of these, about 100 have separate courts of quarter sessions, and about 200 a separate commission of the peace. The population of 89, is under 5,000, and of 18 over 100,000. The quarter sessions boroughs exclude some of the largest, *e.g.*, Sunderland, (pop. 116,548,) and include some of the smaller, *e.g.*, Hythe, (pop. 4,173.) As to overlapping of boundaries, see notes to Chs. I.—III.

Note (*c*). It is not easy to determine in what cases the county justices are *County Juris-* excluded from acting and levying a county rate in boroughs not having separate *diction.* quarter sessions.

The commission of the peace for a county (or riding or division, &c.) *primâ facie* extends over the whole county, &c., except liberties (which have separate justices by commission, charter or usage), and excluding counties of cities or of towns. In the case of a borough (not being a county of a city or of a town or a liberty), the rule seems to be that at common law the jurisdiction of the county justices cannot be excluded unless by an express non-intromittant clause (*ita quod justiciarii comitatus se non intromittant*) in the charter of the borough or in a separate commission granted to it. (2 Hale, P. C. 47 ; 2 Strange, 1154 ; *Talbot* v. *Hubble*, 3 T. R. 279 ; *Blankney* v. *Winstanley*, 4 T. R. 451 ; *R.* v. *Sainsbury*, 4 M. & Sel. 429.) As regards municipal boroughs, the Act of 1882 (s. 154) provides, on the one hand, that where no separate Court of Quarter Sessions has been granted, the county justices shall have jurisdiction, and on the other hand that where such a court has been granted, any part of the borough which before 1835 was exempt from their jurisdiction exercisable out of quarter sessions shall continue exempt. Probably the first enactment overrides any ancient non-intromittant clause, and probably the second enactment implies that boroughs formerly subject to the county justices shall (except as regards county rates) continue subject to them. (But see *R.* v. *Deane*, 2 Q. B. 96.)

In some cases the borough justices have by the charter (or perhaps even by usage) a jurisdiction beyond the borough. (See the cases cited above.)

Recorder.

Note (*d*). A Court of Quarter Sessions may exist without a recorder, or a recorder without a Quarter Sessions. In the former case (*qu.* only Haverfordwest,) the Quarter Sessions are held (as in a county) by the justices. In the latter (*e.g.* Durham, Wells) the recorder is merely the judge of a civil court, or his office is only honorary. Under some Acts, appeals from the justices in a borough having a separate Court of Quarter Sessions are to be made, not to that court, but to the County Quarter Sessions. See *e.g.*, the Licensing Act, 1828 (c. 61, s. 27).

Counties of Towns.

Note (*e*). Besides the three classes of boroughs treated of above, there is a fourth class, viz., boroughs which are themselves separate counties. This class is not now of much legal importance, as such boroughs are for imperial purposes (*e.g.*, militia and assizes) usually deemed part of the adjoining county at large, and for local government purposes do not differ materially from quarter sessions boroughs. Each of them has, however, a sheriff of its own.

The counties of cities are—
Bristol,
Canterbury,
Chester,
Exeter,
Gloucester,
Lichfield,
Lincoln,
London,
Newcastle,
Norwich,
Worcester,
York.

The counties of towns are—
Berwick (1836, c. 103),
Carmarthen,
Haverfordwest,
Hull,
Nottingham,
Poole,
Southampton.

Oxford has also a sheriff of its own.

CHAPTER V.

URBAN DISTRICTS.

(1) *Area of Local Government District.*
(2) *Organization.*
(3) *Purposes and Expenses of Local Boards.*
(4) *Improvement Act Districts.*
(5) *Other Urban Districts.*

BESIDES boroughs there are other urban organizations for purposes of local government. Of these the most numerous are "Local Government Districts," constituted under the Public Health Act, 1875, or the previous sanitary Acts which it repealed. {LOCAL BOARDS. (1) AREA. 1875, c. 55, superseding 1848, c. 63, and 1858, c. 98.}

There are 688 of these districts in England and Wales (including some, *e.g.*, Oxford, which are also municipal boroughs). Their populations are often very small, and sometimes very large, varying from 187 (Childwall, Lancashire) to 128,953 (West Ham, Essex). Their areas frequently cut the area of the poor-law parish, and not seldom that of the union and the county. Their existence has been determined partly by a desire to escape highway expenditure, partly by the non-existence, until the last few years, of any efficient sanitary laws for rural places, sometimes by the desire to escape inclusion in other urban districts. Their areas have naturally been in many cases determined or modified by the opposition of the owners or occupiers of particular properties (*a*).

The Public Health Act, 1875, gives various powers to the Local Government Board for the alteration or combination of existing local government districts; but these powers can in general be exercised only with the consent of the local authorities concerned, or by provisional order, or under both restrictions. New districts cannot be made except by the Local Government Board. That Board may constitute them without the aid of parliament, if the inhabitants of a district vote for such constitution. Without such vote they may be constituted by provisional order, confirmed by parliament. {1875, ss. 270—304.}

(2) Organization.

Local government districts are governed by incorporated local boards, the number of whose members is alterable by the Local Government Board. The members are elected and hold office for three years, retiring annually by thirds (*b*). They may be divided into wards, and when this is the case a number of members is assigned to and separately elected in each ward.

The qualification for members of the Board is as follows:—In a district with less than 20,000 population, £500 property or £15 rating. In a district with 20,000 population or upwards, £1,000 property or £30 rating. And, in either case, residence within seven miles. The property or occupation may be either sole or joint.

The qualification for an elector is his being an "owner" or "ratepayer" in the district. Under the term "owner" is included every person occupying property rateable to the poor-rate at less than a rack rent. The election is by voting papers, and the voting is plural at the rate of one vote for every £50 rating, or part thereof, up to six votes (*c*).

(3) Purposes of Organization.

The purposes of this organization are the "sanitary purposes" of the Public Health Act, 1875, and subsequent Acts. They also include in certain cases the enforcement of the Elementary Education Acts, and the execution of the Burial Acts (*d*).

The expenses of local boards are defrayed for the most part out of a rate called the general district rate, which differs from the poor rate in this, that agricultural land, railways, canals, and tithes are assessed at only one-fourth part of their full rateable value.

(4) Improvement Act Districts.

"Improvement Act districts" are districts constituted under local Acts for purposes generally similar to those of the "local government districts." They are governed by trustees or commissioners elected or appointed in various ways according to the provisions of the special Act (*e*). They are about forty-four in number (including some, *e.g.*, Cambridge, which are also municipal boroughs).

1863, c. 97.

The authorities of local government or improvement act districts with 25,000 population have power under the Stipendiary Magistrates Act, 1863, to petition the Secretary of State for the appointment of a salaried police magistrate. Such magistrate is appointed by the Crown and paid out of the sanitary rate.

(5) Other Urban Districts.
1833, c. 90.

Besides the above there are also certain semi-urban places which have a rudimentary urban organization under the Lighting and Watching Act, 1833. (See Appendix, p. 110.) There are also port sanitary authorities under the Public Health Act. (See Ch. VII.)

NOTES.

Note (*a*). The largest proportion of local government districts (about 200) are in Lancashire and Yorkshire. Of these 71 have a population under 3000 and 11 under 1000. It is thus apparent that many so-called "urban" districts are really rural in character. As an instance of cross boundaries, we may quote Mossley in Lancashire, which comprises parts of four poor-law parishes, two unions, and three counties.

Note (*b*). The council of a borough wholly or partly included within the district of a local board formed between 1848 and 1858, have the right to nominate a certain number of members of the board, but these members are only to hold office for one year, or as long as they continue councillors. The number and qualification of the members of these boards is also somewhat different.
1875, Sched II. 71.
1848, c. 63, ss. 12—16.

Note (*c*). In the election of a local board the owner and the occupier (being separate persons) may each vote in respect of the same premises. A person being both owner and occupier may vote in each capacity in respect of the same premises. Partners more than six in number can only vote as one owner. If not more than six they may each vote as if each were the separate owner of an equal share. It does not appear how partners are to exercise the occupation franchise. Owners must claim annually and be registered.

Note (*d*). For "sanitary" and other purposes, see Chs. VII., XII., XIII., and Appendix, pp. 109—114.

Note (*e*). Local Improvement Acts usually incorporate some of the provisions of the Towns' Improvement Clauses Act, 1847 (relating to sewerage, drainage, paving, cleansing, building regulations, nuisances, gas and water supply, &c.), and of the Towns' Police Clauses Act, 1847 (relating to street traffic, cabs, fires, &c.), or, if passed after 1875, apply the corresponding provisions of the Public Health Act, with such modifications as the circumstances of the locality may require.
1847, c. 34.
c. 89.

B. *Matters which are Locally Administered.*

CHAPTER VI.

POOR-LAW ADMINISTRATION.

(1) *Poor Relief.*
(2) *Settlement.*
(3) *Expenses and Rate.*

(1) POOR RELIEF.
1601, c. 2.
1661, c. 12.
1819, c. 12.
1834, c. 76.
1842, c. 57.
1844, c. 101.
1846, c. 66.
1847, c. 109.
1848, c. 110.
1849, c. 103.
1850, c. 101.
1851, c. 105.
1865, c. 79.
1866, c. 113.
1867, c. 106.
1868, c. 122.
1871, c. 70.
    c. 108.
1874, c. 54.
1876, c. 61.
1879, c. 6.
    c. 54.
1882, c. 36.
    c. 58.

1601, s. 6.
1834, ss. 56, 78.
1848, s. 8.
1882, c. 75, ss. 20, 21.

THE unit for purposes of poor relief is everywhere the "Union" (including a parish organized as a union) and the authority is the guardians of the union. The organization of the union has been already sufficiently explained. (See Ch. II.)

The principle of the poor-laws may be shortly stated thus :—Every person who is unable to support himself has a right to relief, in the first instance in the place in which he is, and then in the place to which he is legally removable ; and such relief is to be administered by boards of guardians and overseers subject to the control and regulations of the Local Government Board, the money being raised by rates levied on real property.

Poor relief is given by the guardians, except in case of urgent necessity, when an overseer may relieve, or on the refusal of an overseer, a justice. The value of relief so given may be recovered from those persons who are liable to maintain the person relieved. The parents, grand-parents, children, and grand-children of a pauper are all liable for his maintenance, but a man is primarily liable to support his wife and children, and a widow, unmarried woman, or married woman with separate property is similarly liable to support her children or husband and children, as the case may be.

Poor relief is given either in or out of the workhouse, but no out-relief may be given except in accordance with Statute or Order of the Local Government Board.

Out-relief may be legally given in various forms: viz., in money or kind (bread, clothes, &c.), in medicine or surgical appliances, by apprenticing or assisting to educate children, by allotting land or aiding

emigration. The payment of school fees by guardians, under the Elementary Education Act, 1876, for the children of non-paupers, is not to be deemed poor relief.
1876, c. 79, s. 10.

In-relief is given inside the workhouses, one or more of which now exist in nearly every union. Under the old Poor Law Acts the churchwardens and overseers of each parish were bound to provide "houses of dwelling for the impotent poor." And now the Local Government Board, with the consent of the guardians of a union or parish, may order a workhouse to be built, and may without such consent, order an existing workhouse to be enlarged and altered, and may also authorise loans (within certain statutory limits) to be raised by the guardians for these and like purposes. A workhouse is managed by the guardians subject to the regulations of the Local Government Board. Besides the regular inmates, the Poor Laws provide for the relief of the wayfaring poor in casual wards, subject, however, in their case to certain liabilities to detention and forced labour. Instead of (or in addition to) providing a workhouse the guardians may contract for the support of their paupers in the workhouse of another union. They may also board out pauper children and send them to schools certified by the Local Government Board, and may provide hospitals and dispensaries for the poor. (As to district schools and pauper lunatics, see Ch. XI., XII.)

1601, s. 4.
1834, ss. 23—25.

1834, s. 42.

1871, c. 108.
1882, c. 36.

The place in which a poor person is entitled to be *permanently* relieved is the place in which he has a settlement, or (if he is irremovable) the place in which he is resident at the time of becoming chargeable. If a pauper is "removable," the guardians of the union to which he becomes chargeable may obtain an order of removal from the justices to send him back to his place of settlement.

(2) SETTLEMENT.

1834, s. 79.
1865, s. 2.

The law of settlement depends on many statutes and judicial decisions, but has been much simplified by recent legislation. Speaking generally, it is as follows:

See especially 1876, ss. 34, 36.

(i.) A person becomes irremovable from (*i.e.*, entitled to permanent relief in) a parish after one year's residence.

(ii.) A person acquires a settlement in a parish after three years' residence.

(iii.) In many cases a person possessing landed property or paying rates may acquire a settlement by a residence of only 40 days.

(iv.) A woman on marriage takes her husband's settlement if that is known.

(v.) No child under 16 can acquire a settlement, but takes its settlement from its father (if legitimate) or mother (if illegitimate or its father is dead), and, after attaining 16, retains that settlement until it acquires another. If its parents' settlement is not known, it takes its settlement from the place of its birth.

Though the parish is still the legal unit of settlement, yet the "union" is practically the unit since the Union Chargeability Act of 1865, which spread the expenses of poor relief over the wider area, and thus deprived the law of settlement of much of its former importance.

(3) EXPENSES. 1865, ss. 1, 9.

The cost of poor relief is now under the Union Chargeability Act (which applies to all unions under the Act of 1834, and may be applied to any union under a local Act by order of the Local Government Board) almost entirely chargeable on the common fund of the union (*a*) (*b*). This fund is formed by contributions from the several parishes within the union in proportion to their rateable value as determined by the last valuation list. (As to valuation, see Ch. XV.) The parish contributions are raised by the poor rate levied by the overseers on the precept of the guardians.

Poor Rate.
1836, c. 96.
1862, c. 103.
1869, c. 41, s. 17.

The poor-rate is levied by a uniform assessment or poundage on the net rateable value of all the lands, houses and mines in the parish. The overseers when proceeding to make a poor-rate, copy the valuation list or the former poor-rate, with amendments, adding to it a statement of the number of shillings or pence in the pound which will produce the required sum, and a column showing the amount to be paid by each occupier, and another column for arrears and sums excused. The document so filled up is properly called an "assessment." A declaration of its correctness is signed by the overseers, and it is submitted to justices for their allowance (which cannot be withheld if the rate is in proper form). When allowed it becomes a "rate", and it must be published and inspection of it must be permitted to ratepayers and certain authorities. The amount due from any person ought to be demanded in writing (*c*) (*d*).

1840, c. 69 (continued by subsequent Acts).
1874, c. 54.

The poor-rate was originally in theory a contribution by inhabitant occupiers according to their ability, and not only land but stock-in-trade was rated in many places. The rating of stock-in-trade has ceased since 1840. It is believed that shipping is still rated in one or two places by local custom or local acts. The Rating Act, 1874, made plantations and woods, rights of sporting and mines of every description rateable to the poor and other local rates. Woods, stone quarries and mines other than coal mines, had been previously rateable for highway purposes only (*e*).

NOTES.

Note (a). (i.) The following expenses are now all chargeable on the common fund of a union :—   *Common fund.* 1834. 1862.
    workhouse and establishment charges,   1865, c. 79,
    relief of poor (both indoor and outdoor),   s. 40.
    vaccination and registration expenses,   1879, c. 6.
    expenses of assessment and school attendance committees,
    election of guardians (general expenses),
    prosecutions by guardians,
    audit stamps,
    charges of pauper lunatics, settled in or irremovable from the union.

(ii.) Among the few items of expenditure still chargeable to separate parishes are—
    salaries of parish collectors and assistant overseers,
    special expenses of contested elections of guardians,
    school fees paid by guardians for children of non-paupers,
    overseers' expenses in respect of jury lists, and of registration of voters.   1844, c. 101, s. 60.

N.B.—The common fund for education purposes is separate from the common poor fund.

Note (b). The expenditure in 1881-2 on poor-law purposes in England and Wales (excluding the metropolis), was as follows :—   *Expenditure.*

In-maintenance	£1,261,603
Outdoor relief	2,427,618
Lunatics.	837,065
Workhouse loans, &c.	205,641
Salaries, &c.	820,373
Miscellaneous	589,224
Total	£6,141,524

Note (c). Poor and all local rates are ordinarily paid by the occupier of the lands, &c. on which they are leviable. But in the case of small house property, it has been found necessary (in order to save excessive inconvenience and expense) to make the owners "compound," *i.e.*, pay rates instead of the occupiers, on being allowed a reasonable reduction. Thus under the Act of 1869 owners of tenements rated at not more than £8 (higher limits are allowed in London, Liverpool, Manchester and Birmingham) may by agreement with the vestry compound at a reduction of 25 per cent., or may be compelled by the vestry to compound at a reduction which may amount to 30 per cent. (*i.e.*, 15 per cent. if the rates are only paid on occupied tenements, with a further deduction not exceeding 15 per cent. more, if the owners agree to pay rates on all their tenements whether occupied or not). The occupiers'   *Compounding.* 1819, c. 12. 1869, c. 41.

names are to be inserted in the rate, and they are qualified as parliamentary or municipal voters, &c., as if they paid the rate. And under the Act of 1819 (not applicable in a parliamentary borough) a vestry may enforce compounding by the owners of dwellings let for terms less than a year or at shorter than quarterly rents, the rents being not less than £6 nor more than £20. The composition may be at one-half the rent or more.

See 1882, c. 27. The power of compelling composition under the Act of 1869 is now made applicable also to highway rates.

Rating of Owners.

1869, c. 41.
cp. 1875, c. 55, s. 214.

1874, c. 54.

Note (d). In recent Acts there has been a growing disposition to relieve occupiers at the expense of owners from the burden of rates, especially when the rate is a new one, or the occupier's term is short. Thus by the Poor Rate Assessment Act of 1869, occupiers for terms of not more than three months may deduct poor rates paid by them from their rents, and by the Rating Act, 1874, ss. 5, 7, occupiers of woods and mines are allowed to make similar deductions. Section 6 of the latter Act, relating to sporting rights, is an instance of owners being rated directly.

Exemptions.

Note (e). There are some exemptions from liability to the poor-rate.

(i.) See—

1814, c. 170, s. 11, as to the power of justices with the consent of the overseers to excuse indigent persons.

1822, c. 126, as to turnpike tolls and houses.

1833, c. 30, as to churches and certified chapels, so far as used exclusively for religious services or for Sunday or charitable schools.

1843, c. 36, as to certified scientific and literary societies.

1854, c. 104, as to lighthouses and property occupied by the Board of Trade.

1863, c. 65, as to volunteer storehouses.

1869, c. 40. Power to rating authorities to exempt premises used exclusively for Sunday or ragged schools without profit.

1853, c. 97, s. 35.
1855, c. 128, s. 15.

(ii.) Lands acquired for lunatic asylums or cemeteries are not at any time to be assessed at a higher value than their assessed value when so acquired.

(iii.) Lands, &c., in the occupation of the Crown or Government are not rateable, but a contribution (amounting in 1882–3 to about £165,000) is now voted in lieu of rates.

(iv.) Some local Acts contain particular exemptions.

Several of the above exemptions extend to other rates besides the poor-rate. See also the Lands Clauses Consolidation Act, 1845, c. 18, s. 133 (and many similar provisions in local Acts), by which railway and other companies are bound to make good deficiencies of rates during the progress of their works.

CHAPTER VII.

SANITARY PURPOSES.

(1) *Sanitary purposes.*
(2) *Areas.*
(3) *Difference between Urban and Rural Sanitary Districts.*
(4) *Divisions of Districts.*
(5) *Port Sanitary Authorities.*

"SANITARY purposes," within the meaning of the Public Health Act, 1875, comprise a great variety of objects which may be roughly classified as follows:— *(1) SANITARY PURPOSES. 1875, c. 55.*

A. Urban authorities only.
- (i.) Town improvements (new streets, bridges, parks, markets, &c.). — ss. 146—148, 164—170.
- (ii.) Lighting. — ss. 161—163.
- (iii.) Maintenance, cleansing and improvement of streets and roads. — ss. 42—47, 144—160.
- (iv.) Regulation of traffic, hackney carriages, fires, &c. — ss. 171, 172.

B. Urban and rural authorities.
- (v.) Water supply. — ss. 51—70.
- (vi.) Sewerage and drainage. — ss. 13—34.
- (vii.) Inspection and prevention of nuisances, (including cellar dwellings, smoke abatement, pollution of rivers, &c). — ss. 71—119.
- (viii.) Provision of hospitals, cemeteries, and mortuaries, and powers in respect of infectious diseases (*a*). — ss. 46, 120—143, 1879, c. 31.

For sanitary purposes the whole country is divided into urban sanitary districts and rural sanitary districts. Every borough, local board district, or improvement act district, is constituted an urban sanitary district. Every rural union, or, in the case of a union which is partly urban and partly rural, so much of it as is rural, is constituted a rural sanitary district (*b*). *(2) AREAS.*

In an urban sanitary district the sanitary authority is the town council, or the local board, or the improvement commissioners, as the case may be. In a rural sanitary district the sanitary authority is the board of guardians (c).

(3) Difference between Urban and Rural Sanitary Districts.

The main difference between urban and rural sanitary districts is that in urban districts provision is made for all the above-mentioned eight classes of sanitary purposes, whereas in a rural district the sanitary authority is authorized to provide only for the four last classes (marked B), or, in other words, it has no control over roads, cannot regulate buildings, cannot light, cannot make improvements, and has no general powers of regulation (d). Again, in urban districts expenses for sanitary purposes are, generally speaking, borne by a rate called the "general district rate," which differs from poor-rates and borough-rates in this important respect, that agricultural land, railways, canals and tithes, &c. are rateable only to the extent of one-fourth of their rateable value—an exemption granted on the ground that they may not be benefited equally with houses and manufactories by town improvements, &c. In rural districts, a similar exemption is allowed as regards "special expenses," but other expenses are, generally speaking, borne out of the poor-rates without the three-fourths exemption (e).

(4) Division of Districts.
Urban.
s. 216.

An urban authority may subdivide its district or any street in the district for any of the purposes of the Act, and may levy a rate specially on any part. The excluded part of a parish which is partly in an urban district, may, within six months from the constitution of the urban district, make itself a separate highway parish; but otherwise it is for highway purposes to be treated as forming part of the urban district, unless it has been included in or formed into a rural highway district.

Rural.
ss. 229, 230, 277.

In a rural sanitary district, each parish is *primâ facie* a separate "contributory place," and is separately chargeable with its own "special expenses," *i.e.*, the expense of providing it separately with water or sewerage, or the expense of any other separate works, or any other expense which the Local Government Board declare to be special (f). These expenses are payable out of a special rate, which is a poor-rate, but is levied in the particular parish or place on the same basis as that of the general district rate of an urban district. "General expenses" are all other expenses of the rural sanitary authority, such as the expenses of the sanitary officer, and are payable out of the common fund of the union raised out of the poor-rates of the several parishes in proportion to their valuations (g).

(5) Port Sanitary Authorities.

The Local Government Board has power to constitute by provisional order any sanitary authority whose district forms part of or abuts on a "port" or any commissioners having authority in a "port," the "port sanitary authority." The order may also combine two or more of such local authorities (called "riparian authorities,") into a joint board to act as the port sanitary authority for one or more "ports." A "port" is any place so appointed by the Treasury for customs purposes under the Act of 1876.

ss. 287—292.

1876, c. 55, s. 11.

The district of a port sanitary authority consists of the waters of the port and so much of the districts of the constituent riparian authorities as are named in the provisional order. A port sanitary authority may be invested with any powers given by the Public Health Act, and may delegate its powers to any of the riparian authorities. Subject to the provisional order, the expenses are defrayed as other sanitary expenses, or, where there is a joint board, out of a common fund to which the riparian authorities contribute in proportions fixed by the Local Government Board (*h*).

NOTES.

Note (*a*). For sanitary purposes not included in the Public Health Act, see Appendix, pp. 109—114.

Other Sanitary purposes.

Note (*b*). The following is a rough estimate (in millions) of the number, size, population and rateable value of urban and rural sanitary districts (excluding the metropolis).

Number, &c., of areas.

Number.	Acreage.	Population.	Rateable value.
			£
985 U. S. D.	2½ millions.	14 millions	56 millions.
575 R. S. D.	34½ millions	8½ millions.	56½ millions.

This would give for each rural sanitary authority an average area of about 60,000 acres, population of 15,000, and rateable value of £98,000. Some of the fragments which remain as rural sanitary districts, after taking out of the unions the urban areas, are very minute. For instance, the residual rural sanitary district in the Reading union appears to have only 1440 population, that in the Birkenhead union 390, that in the Derby union 995.

Note (*c*). To the general rules as to sanitary authorities given above there are many exceptions, the principal of which are the following:—

Exceptions.

1875, s. 6.	(i.) Any urban district which is wholly included in a larger urban district is merged in the larger district, and is for "sanitary purposes" subject to the sanitary authority of the larger district.
(ii.) When a local board district and an improvement act district coincide, the latter is merged.
(iii.) When a local board district cuts a borough, or an improvement act district cuts a borough or a local board district, the part outside the borough continues to be governed as before the Act until altered by provisional order.
(iv.) Oxford, Cambridge, Blandford, Calne, Wenlock, Folkestone and Newport (Isle of Wight), are specially treated.
	And as to authorities in rural districts—
s. 9.	(i.) In a union part of which is included in one or more urban districts, an *ex officio* guardian resident in an urban part cannot act as a member of the rural authority unless qualified for election by property or occupation in the rural part, and an elective guardian for a wholly urban parish cannot act as a member of the rural authority.
(ii.) If a parish is partly in an urban and partly in a rural part of the union, the Local Government Board may divide the parish into urban and rural wards, with separate guardians.
(iii.) If a rural authority is reduced by these provisions to fewer than five guardians, the Local Government Board may make them up to five by nomination of persons qualified for election.
Urban Powers in Rural Districts. s. 276.	**Note (d).** The Local Government Board have power on application to invest a rural authority with any of the powers of an urban authority either for their whole district, or any contributory place. This power has been extensively exercised, no less than 444 such orders having been made down to 1882 (L. G. B. Report 1883, p. 89). A rural sanitary authority may also be invested with highway powers under the Highway Act of 1878 (see Ch. VIII.).
Rates.	**Note (e).** The Public Health Act contains the following special provisions as to rates:—
ss. 6, 207.	(i.) In a borough in which the "sanitary" expenses were, before 1875, paid otherwise than out of the borough fund or rate, they are (subject to the provisions of local acts) to be paid out of a general district rate. But in other boroughs they are paid out of the borough rate without the three-fourths exemptions.
(ii.) In an improvement act district in which such expenses were paid out of a rate in the nature of a general district rate leviable over the whole district, they continue to be so paid.
s. 216.	(iii.) In an urban district, if the whole district is without public works of paving, water supply and sewerage, roads are to be maintained out of a highway rate. If part is without such works, the roads in that part are to be maintained out of a special highway rate on that part.
s. 203.	(iv.) In an urban district, where in 1875 the expenses were not payable out of a general district rate, the Local Government Board may on application declare them so payable, subject to the exceptional highway provisions.
ss. 213, 232.	(v.) Private improvement rates may also be levied on individual occupiers both in urban and rural districts.

Note (*f*). Any area consisting of several parishes or parts of parishes, may be constituted by the Local Government Board a separate "contributory place" (also called a "special drainage district") and becomes separately chargeable with "special expenses." *Contributory place.* ss. 229, 277.

Note (*g*). For further details of expenditure for sanitary purposes in 1881-82, see Table F. (p. 88). *Expenditure.*

Note (*h*). In 1883 there were in England and Wales (excluding London) 45 port sanitary authorities, 8 being joint boards. Their total expenditure amounted to about £9000 for the year ending March 1882. *Port authorities.*

[N.B.—*This Chapter only refers to England and North Wales. A Note on the South Wales Road System is appended* (p. 40).]

CHAPTER VIII.

HIGHWAYS.

(1) *The Highway "parish."*
(2) *The Highway district.*
(3) *Roads under sanitary authorities.*
(4) *Turnpikes.*
(5) *Main roads.*

THERE are three principal kinds of highway areas :—(1) the highway "parish," (2) the highway district, (3) the district of an urban or rural sanitary authority exercising highway powers.

There are also three classes of roads:—(1) the ordinary "highway," (2) the "main road," (3) the turnpike road. Of these the first class are administered exclusively by the local authorities of the above-mentioned areas; the second by those authorities in conjunction with the county authority; while the third are under trusts, but have become in recent years, from the causes explained below, largely dependent for maintenance on the highway rates.

(1) HIGHWAY PARISH.
1835, c. 50.
1841, c. 51.
1845, c. 71.
1876, c. 62.
1878, c. 77.
1879, c. 39.
1882, c. 27.

There are now about 6,203 parishes separately maintaining their own highways under the Parish Highways Act, 1835, and amending Acts.

This Act *applies* of itself to every rural parish in England and Wales which is not included in any Highway District. It must be observed that in this and the other Highway Acts "parish" has not the same meaning as in the Poor Law Acts, but includes many hamlets, villages, tithings, &c., which are not separate poor-law parishes (*a*). The ordinary *organization* provided by this Act is very imperfect. It does not constitute any board, except in the special case mentioned below, but merely provides for the appointment of a parish surveyor, elected by the persons rateable for Highway expenses, with a provision for appointment by the justices at quarter or special sessions of one joint surveyor for a group of consenting parishes. The special exception mentioned above is that of parishes with over 5,000 population. In these the Vestry may elect a Highway Board to do the work of surveyors, and such Board may appoint a clerk, assistant surveyor, and collectors of rates. With this exception (which now only applies to a few parishes) it may be said that the whole machinery provided by the Act consists of a surveyor.

The *functions* of the surveyor are the maintenance and repair of the parish roads, exclusive of turnpikes and of roads governed by local Acts.

The *expenses* are paid out of a separate Highway-rate, levied by the surveyor upon property liable to the Poor-rate, subject to customary exemptions (*b*). The limit of the rate is 2*s*. 6*d*. in the £. But additional special rates can be made for compensations, law expenses, &c. Where a joint surveyor is appointed for several "parishes," a separate surveyor must still be appointed in each of the "parishes" for rating purposes. 1835, ss. 27-35.

There are now about 362 districts, composed of about 7,886 rural "parishes," combined for highway purposes under the District Highways Acts, 1862 and 1864, and amending Acts.

These Acts *apply* only where Quarter Sessions so order on the application of five justices of a proposed district. On such application the Quarter Sessions may constitute a Highway district by combining any number of Highway "parishes." South Wales, the Isle of Wight, urban districts, and places under local road Acts are excluded from these Acts. The adoption of these Acts has been both partial and unsystematic. In forming Highway Districts the justices sometimes chose the union area, more often the petty sessional division. In many cases they constituted a special area, thus adding to the confusion of Local Government. Many small towns and populous villages avoided the operation of the Highway Acts by adopting the Local Government Acts. Some counties again are entirely "districted," some have always resisted the formation of Highway districts, and in others districts have been dissolved owing to the dissatisfaction of the ratepayers with the working of the Act of 1878 (*c*).

(2) Highway District.
1862, c. 61.
1863, c. 61.
1864, c. 101.
1878, c. 77.
1879, c. 39.
1882, c. 27.

The *organization* provided by these Acts consists of a District Highway Board composed of the justices resident in the district, and of waywardens elected by the several parishes, the number of the waywardens for each parish being fixed by the Quarter Sessions. The Board must appoint a treasurer, clerk and district surveyor, but a joint surveyor may be appointed for several Boards.

The *functions* of the Board as regards the repair and maintenance of roads are generally similar to those of surveyors under the Act of 1835.

The *expenses* are (since 1878) borne by the common or district fund, but in exceptional circumstances, such as a difference of soil, a Highway Board may with the consent of the county Quarter Sessions 1878, c. 77, s. 7.

divide its districts into two or more parts (each consisting of integral highway parishes) and charge separately to each such part the expenses of maintaining its own highways. The Common or District Fund is formed by contributions in proportion to the Poor Law valuations of the several parishes. The amount of the contribution so due from a "parish," and that of its separate charges for its own roads, are levied by a precept. If the "parish" is not a Poor Law parish, or if for seven years before 1862 it had a separate Highway-rate more extensive in incidence than the Poor-rate, the precept goes to the waywardens, and the amount is raised by them by a separate Highway-rate. In other cases the precept goes to the overseers, and they pay out of the Poor-rate. The limit in either case is 2s. 6d. in the £, unless four-fifths of the ratepayers consent to more.

<small>1864, ss. 32, 33.</small>

By the Public Health Act, 1875, every urban sanitary authority is the exclusive highway authority within its district, with special powers in respect of bridges, new roads, &c. (d).

<small>(3) SANITARY AUTHORITIES.
I. Urban.
1875, c. 55, ss. 144, 216. Sched. V., Part III.</small>

The *expenses* are primâ facie chargeable on the general district rate, with the three-fourths exemption for agricultural land, &c. But there are important exceptions: *e.g.*, expenses heretofore borne by the borough fund or rate (which has no three-fourths exemption) are to continue to be so borne; and where only part of a district is rated for paving, water, sewerage, &c., the highways in the other part are to be paid for out of a separate Highway-rate on that other part; and where there are no public water or sewerage works in the district, the highways are to be paid for out of a separate Highway-rate over the whole district.

<small>II. Rural.</small>

Rural sanitary authorities do not as a rule exercise any highway powers, but in 30 districts comprising some 577 highway "parishes" (included in the 7,886 districted parishes mentioned above), the guardians have been invested with highway powers under the Highways and Locomotives Act, 1878.

<small>1878, c. 77, ss. 3—5.</small>

Under this Act any rural sanitary authority of a district, co-incident in area with a highway district formed under the Acts of 1862 and 1864, may be authorized by an order of the "county authority" (*i.e.*, the justices in Quarter Sessions of the county or counties in which the district is situated), to exercise all the powers of a Highway Board. On such order being made, the Highway Board is *ipso facto* dissolved, and their property, liabilities, &c., pass to the rural sanitary authority, who defray all highway expenses as general sanitary expenses under the Public Health Act. In order to facilitate future amalgamations of this kind, the Act of 1878 directs the county authority in forming or altering highway districts under the Highway

Acts, to make them as far as possible coincide with rural sanitary districts.

In certain places also the guardians exercise control over rural roads under the provisions of the Public Health Act, 1875, which empower the Local Government Board to invest any rural sanitary authority with highway powers in respect of the whole or part of the sanitary district. In this case the expenses are paid as other sanitary expenses (See Ch. VII. p. 30). 1875, c. 55, s. 276.

The provisions of the numerous Turnpike Acts, so far as they relate to the constitution, powers, liabilities and dissolution of trusts, are not material for the present purpose. But the gradual lapse of Turnpike Trusts into insolvency through the falling off in their tolls has during the last 40 years had an important bearing on the finance and law of Highways. By the Acts of 1841 and 1863, the justices in special sessions were empowered to order contributions from the Highway-rates of parishes and districts towards the repair of turnpikes with insufficient tolls. Turnpike roads ceasing to be so, became ordinary highways, and the expenses of their maintenance have since 1870 been charged in districts on the common fund. Under Acts of 1872 and 1873, and the Public Health Act (s. 148) District Boards or urban sanitary authorities may voluntarily take over turnpikes in their districts.

(4) TURNPIKES. 1841, c. 59. 1863, c. 94. 1865, c. 107. 1870, c. 73. 1871, c. 115. 1872, c. 85. 1873, c. 90. 1874, c. 95. 1875, ch. cxciv. 1876, c. 39. And see the other annual Turnpike Acts.

Turnpike Trusts are now rapidly disappearing. For the last 30 years Annual Acts have been passed providing for the winding-up and dissolution of a gradually increasing number. In the ten years 1871-81, the number of trusts decreased from 852 to 184. In January, 1883, there remained only 71 trusts, comprising 2180 miles of road, and the terms of nearly (if not quite) all these will have expired at the end of 1893. See L. G. B. Report, 1882—3, p. cxl.

The Highways and Locomotives Act, 1878, was passed chiefly with a view to remedy the great hardship and inconvenience arising from the extensive abolition of turnpike trusts and the consequent lapsing of turnpike roads into ordinary highways. In many of such cases, where there were no highway districts, agricultural parishes had to bear the whole burden of maintaining thoroughfares with heavy traffic between large towns or to or from railway stations. To meet this evil and prevent the deterioration of such thoroughfares, the Act of 1878 created a new class of "main roads."

(5) MAIN ROADS. 1878, c. 77.

See H. C. S. C. Report on Turnpikes, 1875.

These include:—

(i.) All roads ceasing since 1870 to be turnpike roads, except those which the Local Government Board on the application of the "county authority" think fit to "dismain" by provisional order confirmed by Act of Parliament.

(ii.) All roads which, on the application of a "highway authority," are declared by the "county authority," to be main roads.

Main roads are, like ordinary highways, maintained by the "highway authority," but the county authority are to pay out of the county rate half the expenses of maintenance of any main road, certified by the county inspector to be maintained satisfactorily (*e*). The "county authority" are the justices in quarter sessions of a county, or any liberty with a separate rate. The "highway authority" may be either an urban sanitary authority, highway board, or the surveyor of a highway parish maintaining its own roads. Quarter sessions boroughs, and parts of parishes forming part of such boroughs for highway purposes (see note (*d*) below), are outside counties for the purposes of this Act.

Control of county authority.

Under the Act of 1878 the county authority have also had vested in them, for the first time, some general powers of control over highways. Thus they can order any highway authorities, who make default in maintaining their roads (whether main or ordinary highways) to perform their duties, and may, on non-compliance with their order, repair the roads themselves and charge the expenses on the highway rates of the district or parish. The county authority have also certain powers of making bye-laws (subject to confirmation by the Local Government Board) for regulating the use both of main roads and highways, and of licensing locomotives (*f*).

1878, c. 77, ss. 26, 32, 35.

In March, 1881, there were 15,190 miles of main roads in England and North Wales (including those within urban districts), to which the county authority contributed a sum of £316,000, representing half the cost of maintenance. Since 1882 another quarter of the cost of maintaining main roads has been repaid to the "highway authorities" out of the Parliamentary votes (*g*).

NOTES.

"*Highway parish.*"

1862, s. 7.
1864, ss. 5—9.
1875, s. 216.
1879, c. 54, s. 7.
1882, c. 27, s. 9.

Note (*a*). Many townships, hamlets, tithings, &c. which are not separate poor-law parishes are separate "highway parishes" by ancient custom. Separate highway parishes are also constituted in many cases by the provisions of the District Highways Acts, and the Public Health Act, 1875. In forming highway districts the justices may constitute any poor law parish a highway parish, and may combine or sever any highway parishes not coincident with poor law parishes. Under the Divided Parishes Acts, 1876, 1879, the Local Government Board may merge detached parts of highway parishes or constitute them separate parishes. That

Board has, however, no general power to make a highway parish co-extensive with a poor law parish.

In 1881 there were, *e.g.*, in Shropshire 740 highway and only 224 poor law parishes. (H. L. S. C. Report on Highways, p. 820.)

Note (*b*). A valuation list made under the Union Assessment Acts is conclusive for the assessment of the highway rate, and where the vestry of a parish have made an order on owners to compound for the poor rate, such order extends to the highway rate. (See Chs. VI., XV., pp. 27, 64.) *Highway rate.* 1882, c. 27.

Note (*c*). In March, 1882, there were 7 counties in England and North Wales with no highway districts, and 5 with no separate highway parishes. Yorkshire had 759 parishes districted and 720 separate. Considerable changes have recently taken place in the districting of highway parishes. One of the results of the Act of 1878 may be traced by a comparison of the numbers of parishes separately maintaining their own highways in 1879 and 1884. This number increased in the five years ending March, 1884, from 5,868 to 6,203, while the number of highway districts correspondingly diminished. *Districts.*

Note (*d*). In the case of a poor law parish, partly within and partly without an urban district, the excluded part may be included in a highway district, or may (by resolution of owners and ratepayers approved by the Local Government Board) be constituted a highway parish, but otherwise such excluded part is to be treated as part of the urban district for rating and all other highway purposes. *Semi-urban districts.* 1875, c. 55, s. 216.

There may be places which are not urban or rural sanitary districts, and yet in which the Highway Acts, are excluded and the roads are vested in the local authority. This may be the case in any place (not being an "urban sanitary district") in which the Towns Improvement Clauses Act, 1847, is in force. 1847, c. 47.

Note (*e*). A "main road" under the Act of 1878, appears to be the whole, or (where the Trust was in two counties or has been partly "dismained") part of an old turnpike trust, and is consequently often not a single line of communication but a group of such lines. (See, however, *Corporation of Rochdale v. Justices of Lancashire*, 8 Q. B. D. 12.) It may be under several highway authorities who have each a separate claim for the county contribution in respect of the part within their district. In certain cases the liability to contribute may be transferred from the county to a hundred liable to repair bridges (s. 20). *Main Roads*

Note (*f*). In addition to the Highway Acts mentioned above there are three Acts relating to the use of locomotives on roads. Those of 1865 and 1878 are only temporary. As to bridges and tramways, see Appendix, pp. 106, 111. *Locomotives.* 1861, c. 70. 1865, c. 83. 1878, c. 77, ss. 28—33.

Note (*g*). The following table shows the mileage and comparative cost of maintenance of highways and main roads in separate parishes and districts for the year 1881—2:— *Highway Expenditure.*

	Mileage.		Cost of Repairs.		Average per Mile.	
	H.	M. R.	H.	M. R.	H.	M. R.
Parishes	38,787	4,660	£477,872	£178,261	£12 6s.	£38 5s.
Districts	55,586	9,800	£705,110	£361,144	£12 13s.	£36 17s.
Total	94,373	14,460	£1,182,982	£539,405	£12 10s.	£37 6s.

The establishment charges were £28,669 in the separate parishes, £69,062 in the districts.

The highway accounts for 1881—2, show a sum of £8,816 contributed to turnpike trusts, and a further sum of £5,798 expended (by highway boards only) on repairs of turnpike roads. There seems no way of estimating accurately either the total cost or the average cost per mile of maintenance of turnpike roads, but there is little doubt that the old system of tolls was more costly than the present system of maintaining main roads out of rates. (See H. L. S. C. Report, p. 882.)

See also the House of Lords S. C. Report on Highways, 1881 (Parliamentary Papers 1881/87), for various suggestions as to the best mode of maintaining highways. A system of local license duties is recommended with much force by Sir E. Harrington, who also suggests a more elaborate sub-division of highways into classes. (Appendix B. to the Report.)

APPENDIX TO CHAPTER VIII.

ROADS IN SOUTH WALES.

In the six southern counties of Wales, the roads are under an exceptional organization, which is of special interest as having formed the precedent for much of the recent highway legislation in England. There are in these counties three classes of roads and three local authorities.

1844, c. 91.
1845, c. 61.
1847, c. 72.
1875, c. 35.
1882, c. 67.

1. *Turnpikes* under a County Roads Board and District Roads Boards. In 1844, all the turnpike roads in a county were transferred to a County Roads Board, composed of 6 to 8 justices elected by quarter sessions with certain ex-officio members and representatives of District Boards. These County Boards have the general control of both turnpike roads and highways. They may continue and discontinue tolls at their discretion (the debt incurred in paying off the creditors being now extinguished). If tolls are discontinued the turnpike road becomes an ordinary highway. In some counties, districts for turnpikes were constituted, and *District Boards* nominated by the Commissioners appointed in 1844. Vacancies on these boards are filled by co-optation, all resident justices being ex officio members. Every District Board sends two representatives to County Roads Board. The District Boards manage the roads within their district and carry out improvements under the superintendence of and with funds and materials supplied by the County Board. *Expenses* are paid out of tolls, and, failing them, out of a county road rate made at quarter sessions like a county rate with contributions from liberties and places exempt from county rate. Rates paid by tenant may be deducted from rent (1844, s. 101). The county road rate is limited in amount and it is not obligatory on the justices to make any (1875). In 1881 the expenditure of County Roads Boards amounted to £27,621, of which £3,136 only was raised by rates.

1835, c. 50.
1860, c. 68.
(See 1851, c. 16.)
1878, c. 34.

2. *Ordinary Highways* under Highway Boards. Every county is divided into highway districts which may be altered by the County Roads Board. Boroughs with a separate commission of the peace may at any time by resolution of the council constitute themselves separate highway districts.

A Highway Board consists of resident justices and guardians elected for poor-law parishes within the district. It appoints its own treasurer and clerk, but the district surveyor is appointed by the County Roads Board. Expenses of maintenance are not (as in England) borne by a common fund, but each parish is charged with the cost of its own highways, a highway rate being levied like the poor rate. Officers' salaries however are charged on the parishes in the districts, in the same proportion as the county rate. A Highway Board may borrow for improvements with approval of the County Roads Board. Subject to the provisions of the later Acts, the Parish Highways Act, 1835, applies to South Wales.

3. *District Roads.* These are a class of roads between turnpikes and ordinary highways. The County Roads Boards may declare any highway, being a main thoroughfare, to be a district road, and thereupon the cost of maintaining such road is to be a common charge on the highway district to be borne by parishes in the same proportion as the county rate. 1878, c. 34, s. 9.

In 1881 the mileage of the South Wales Roads (other than turnpikes) was 7,264, and the average cost of maintenance per mile was less than £6, or less than half the average cost of ordinary highways in England.

CHAPTER IX.

POLICE.

(1) *Ancient Police.*
(2) *County Police.*
(3) *Borough Police.*
(4) *Other Police Forces.*
(5) *Special Constables.*

(1) ANCIENT POLICE.
See 2 Hale, P. C. 96, 97.

The *ancient* Police organization of the country consisted of (i.) a high constable for each hundred or other similar area; (ii.) petty constables (or headboroughs, tithing-men or borsholders) for townships &c.; and (iii.) watchmen appointed in towns under the Statute of Winchester, or appointed in any place by Justices of the Peace *virtute officii*. In more modern times the appointment and duties of parish constables were provided for and regulated by several statutes. The whole of this organization is now practically obsolete (*a*).

MODERN POLICE.

The *modern* Police organization of the country consists mainly of police forces established since 1839 under the County and Borough Police Acts.

(2) COUNTY POLICE.
1839, c. 93.
1840, c. 88.
1856, c. 69.
1857, c. 2.
1858, c. 68.
1859, (2) c. 32.
1865, c. 35.
1875, c. 48.
1876, c. 64.
Area.
1839, 1840, 1856, 1859.

The County Police area is, *primâ facie*, the whole county, including liberties, but excluding all municipal boroughs in which a separate force has been established, and certain other special jurisdictions. Detached fragments of a county are, for Police purposes, merged in the county within which they lie. Adjoining counties may, by agreement, specially adjust their boundaries for Police purposes, so as to include in one Police area the whole of any divided town or place, or otherwise to obviate the inconvenience of irregular boundaries. The Police "county" is thus a different area from the county for other purposes.

Organization.
1839, 1840, 1856.

The Police force for a county consists of a number of men and officers fixed by the Quarter Sessions. A superintendent is appointed for each Petty Sessional Division or other locality, as may be ordered by the Quarter Sessions; and the direction, control, appointment (with approval of two justices) and dismissal of the superintendents, inferior officers and men are vested in a chief constable, who is himself appointed and removable by the Quarter Sessions. The chief constable reports periodically to the Quarter Sessions; the superintendents make reports to Petty Sessions.

The expenses of the County Police force are paid out of a special County Police rate, which is levied over the whole County Police area as above defined on the same basis and valuation as the county rate. In the case of a liberty or other place which is under the County Police, but is not liable to the county rate, the sum due is paid by the treasurer of the liberty or place on a warrant from the county treasurer, and collected by a separate Police rate within the liberty. Down to 1875 a Treasury subvention, limited to one-fourth of the cost of pay and clothing, was made to efficient County Police forces. The limitation has now been temporarily removed and the subvention is now doubled. *Expenses. 1840, 1856.*

In any part of a Police County, districts may be constituted by the Quarter Sessions, and shall be constituted, if so directed by Order in Council, with different numbers of Police, according to their requirements. When a Police county or a part thereof is so districted, the Police rate is to be separately assessed and levied in each district, and the Police expenses of the districted area are divided into the two heads of "general expenditure" and "local expenditure." The local expenditure is to include pay, clothing and such other expenses as the Quarter Sessions direct, and is to be defrayed by the district in and for which it is incurred. The remaining or "general" expenditure is to be defrayed "in common by all the districts." These provisions for districts have probably ceased to be of much importance, since the removal of the limit to Treasury subventions for pay and clothing. *Districts in Counties. 1840, s. 27. 1856, s. 4.*

Though the Quarter Sessions are the Police authority in the county, they are subject, in respect of nearly every part of their Police jurisdiction, to the control of the Secretary of State. His consent or approval is necessary for fixing or altering the numbers of the men and officers, in the selection of the chief constable, for establishing rules for the government and duties of the force (these rules must also be laid before Parliament), for fixing scales of fees and allowances, and for constituting districts and assigning items to the "local expenditure." Moreover, he appoints inspectors, who report to him, and on whose certificate of efficiency the Treasury subvention depends. *Control and Inspection.*

By the Municipal Corporations Act, 1882, the Watch Committee of the Council of every municipal borough must provide for a sufficient number of Police for the borough. The Watch Committee also fix the salaries of the Police with the approval of the Council, and they or any two justices have the power of dismissal. There is no officer or person *(3) Borough Police. 1882, c. 50, ss. 190, 200.*

standing in relation to the Borough Police in the same position in which the chief constable stands to the County Police. The expenses of the Borough Police are paid out of the borough fund or borough rate, or in certain places out of a watch rate which is limited to 8*d*. The boroughs receive a Treasury subvention in the same manner as the counties, and on the same condition of their Police being certified as efficient by the Government Inspector.

Consolidation of forces.

It has been the policy of the Police Acts to encourage a partial "consolidation" of County and Borough Police. With this view the County Police Act of 1840 enables a municipal borough to agree for combination on the terms that the county chief constable shall have the direction and dismissal of the Borough Police; and by the Act of 1856 it is added that such an agreement cannot be terminated without the consent of the Secretary of State, and that a borough with not more than 5,000 population shall not receive any Treasury subvention unless it has so consolidated; and that, on the application of a borough, terms of consolidation may be imposed on a county by Order in Council. It should be observed that the so-called "consolidation"

See 1840, s. 14.

appears not to subject the borough to the County Police rate, but in all other respects (except the appointment of the men) it appears to subject the Borough Police to the same regulations (including control by the County Quarter Sessions and the Secretary of State) as the County Police. Since 1877 no separate police force can be established in a newly incorporated borough with less than 20,000 inhabitants (*b*).

(4) OTHER POLICE FORCES.

Separate Police forces, other than in municipal boroughs, were abolished by the County Police Acts, with the following exceptions:—

1833, c. 90.

(i.) Police forces in large parishes under the Lighting and Watching Act, 1833. It is believed that no such separate forces now exist. If any such forces exist, the Chief Constable of the county can supersede them at his pleasure unless

1856, c. 69, ss. 18, 19.

the population is 15,000, in which case he must get the leave of the Secretary of State.

(ii.) Police forces in places under local Acts. In 1884 there were (outside the Metropolitan Police District) only two such

Hove.
1858, ch. cxx.
Tunbridge Wells.
1846, ch. cccxlix.

places,—Hove and Tunbridge Wells. They are entitled to the Treasury subvention, and may be taken over by the Chief Constable of the county, in the same manner as places under the Lighting and Watching Act (*b*).

Metropolis.
1829, c. 44.
1839, c. 47.
ch. xciv.

The Metropolitan Police and the City of London Police are governed by their local Acts. The whole of Middlesex and parts of Surrey,

Kent, Essex, and Hertford are within the Metropolitan Police District, and the constables of that force have full powers to act within these counties, and also in Berkshire and Buckinghamshire, and on the whole of the lower Thames.

By an Act of 1840 on the application and at the cost of the "company of proprietors of any canal or navigable river," constables may be appointed by two Justices or by the Watch Committee of a borough "to act as constables on and along such canal or river." Their powers are defined, but it does not appear that they are subject to any public authority. *Canals.* 1840, c. 50.

There are also River Police forces under local Acts, *e. g.*, on the Tyne, the Wear, and the Mersey. There is also a partially separate Dockyards Police. *Tyne.* 1852, ch. cx. *Docks.* 1860, c. 135. 1861, c. 51.

To assist the regular police in times of disturbance, Acts of 1831 to 1838 provide for the appointment of Special Constables by county or borough justices in cases where riot or felonies have taken place or are apprehended. And by the Municipal Corporations Act, 1882, provision is made for the annual nomination of Special Constables in municipal boroughs to act when so required by warrant of justices in cases of emergency (*c*). (5) SPECIAL CONSTABLES. 1831, c. 41. 1835, c. 43. 1838, c. 80. 1882, c. 50, s. 196.

NOTES.

Note (*a*). (i.) As to *High Constables*, see 1827, c. 31, 1844, c. 33, s. 8, and 1869, c. 47 (the High Constables Act, 1869), which provides for the abolition of the office, with certain savings. *High and Parish Constables.*

(ii.) As to *Parish Constables*, see 1842, c. 109, 1844, c. 52, 1850, c. 20, and 1872, c. 92 (The Parish Constables Act, 1872), which provides that for the future no parish constable shall be appointed unless by justices on the resolution of the Vestry in a rural parish, or by order of Quarter Sessions, and that if any are so appointed they shall be under the chief constable of the county. Where they are appointed on resolution of a vestry, a salary may be assigned to them by the vestry and is charged on the poor rate. Parishes may combine for such appointments.

Note (*b*). Besides the regular police in counties, boroughs, &c., provision is made for the appointment by the chief constable of a county, with the approval of the Quarter Sessions, of "additional constables" on the application and at the cost of companies or persons. Such Police are under the direction of the chief constable of the county. No Treasury subvention is made towards their cost. They *Additional Constables.*

numbered about 800 in 1882. See the County Police Acts of 1840, s. 19; 1856, s. 15; and see the Towns Police Clauses Act, 1847 (c. 89, s. 7), and the Harbours Clauses Act, 1847 (c. 27, s. 79).

Number of Forces, &c.

Note (*c*). The number of "County" police forces in 1882 was 56, Suffolk being treated for this purpose as two counties, Sussex as two, Yorkshire as three, Cumberland and Westmoreland together as one; Middlesex being thrown into the Metropolitan Police District, and the liberties of Ely and of Peterborough being treated as counties. The number of separate Borough forces in 1882 was 164, and the number of boroughs policed by or consolidated with the counties was about 85. The total number of County, Borough and Local-Act Police in 1882 was 20,244, exclusive of the 800 "additional constables," and apparently also of Canal Police. It appears that of the boroughs with separate police forces, 22 have a population under 5000, and 24 have forces consisting of less than 5 constables apiece. To use the words of one of H.M.'s inspectors of constabulary, "a service thus subdivided cannot be worked to advantage either in respect of efficiency or economy." (Parly. Papers, $\frac{1\,8\,8}{8\,4}$*).

CHAPTER X.

LICENSING.

(1) *Intoxicating liquors.*
(2) *Theatres, &c.*
(3) *Slaughter Houses.*
(4) *Miscellaneous.*

THE areas for licensing are, speaking generally, the county and borough, the county being divided into petty sessional divisions.

In *counties* (including all boroughs with no commission of the peace) the licensing authority for intoxicating liquors are the justices in special or quarter sessions. The justices of each licensing district (*i.e.*, each petty sessional division) hold a general annual licensing meeting for the grant of new licenses, and the renewal or removal of existing licenses, and also several special sessions a year for the transfer of licenses. New licenses and orders sanctioning removals have to be confirmed by the County Licensing Committee appointed by the justices in quarter sessions in their administrative capacity, while appeals against refusals to renew or transfer are heard by the justices in quarter sessions in their judicial capacity.

(1) INTOXICATING LIQUORS.
1828, c. 61.
1869, c. 27.
1870, c. 29.
1872, c. 94.
1874, c. 49.
1880, c. 6.
1882, c. 34.

1872, ss. 37, 50.
1828, s. 27.

In *boroughs* (including counties of cities and towns) with a commission of the peace, the justices are also the licensing authority, and the whole borough the licensing district. Where there are ten or more justices, a committee appointed by the whole body hold the general licensing meetings and sessions for transfers, while the whole body in special sessions confirm the new licenses and removals. In boroughs, with less than ten justices, new licenses, &c. are granted by the whole body, and confirmed by a joint committee appointed by the borough justices and the Licensing Committee of the adjoining county. In all boroughs appeals against refusals to renew and transfer lie to the quarter sessions of the adjoining county, and not to the recorder, who has no licensing jurisdiction.

1872, s. 38.

1828, s. 27.
1882, c. 50, s. 165.

Liberties with separate quarter sessions are "counties" for licensing purposes, but appeals against refusals lie alternatively to the quarter sessions of the adjoining county or of the liberty.

As to the powers of justices in dealing with intoxicating liquor licenses, it should be remembered that they have absolute discretion to grant or refuse any license, renewal, transfer or removal; except that—

(i.) In the case of renewals or transfers of existing licenses, not being beerhouse licenses for consumption *off* the premises, their power to refuse arbitrarily (*i.e.*, without reasonable cause) is doubtful, and an appeal to quarter sessions always lies against their decision ; and,

1869, ss. 8, 19.

(ii.) In the case of beer and wine houses licensed for sale for consumption *on* the premises on May 1st, 1869, they can only refuse renewals on one or other of the four grounds mentioned in the Wine and Beerhouse Act, 1869 (*a*).

Billiards.
1845, c. 109.
1872, c. 94, s. 75.
1880, sess. 2, c. 20, s. 47.

Licenses for billiards (which include the right to sell beer) are granted, renewed, &c. in the same way as intoxicating liquor licenses, but do not require confirmation. There is no appeal against refusals to grant or transfer.

(2) THEATRES, &c.
1843, c. 68.

The authority for licensing buildings for the performance of stage plays (outside the jurisdiction of the Lord Chamberlain) are the justices of a borough or of a petty sessional division of a county. They are on application to hold special sessions for granting licenses, and may also make regulations (subject to approval of the Secretary of State) for securing order and decency in theatres. They have also power to close theatres on breach of regulations, but this is apparently a judicial power similar to the forfeiture of an intoxicating liquor license.

Music, &c.
1752, c. 36.

Within 20 miles of London and Westminster the county justices in quarter sessions must also license places for music and dancing.

(3) SLAUGHTER-HOUSES.
(*a*) 1786, c. 71.
1844, c. 87.
(*b*) 1847, c. 34, ss. 125-131.
1875, c. 55, s. 169.

Slaughter-houses requiring licenses are of two kinds :—

(*a*.) Knackers' premises (not for butchers' meat) have to be licensed annually by the justices in quarter sessions.

(*b*.) Slaughter-houses for butchers' meat are in urban sanitary districts licensed and regulated by the sanitary authority. It seems doubtful whether urban sanitary authorities have also power to regulate knackers' yards.

(4) MISCELLANEOUS.
1831, c. 32.
1839, c. 33.
1871, c. 105.
1879, c. 47.

The justices in special or petty sessions also grant licenses for :—

(i.) Dealing in game.

(ii.) Petroleum (except in urban sanitary districts and harbours where the licensing authority is the sanitary or harbour authority).

(iii.) Explosives (except in a borough or harbour where the town council or harbour authority license).   1875, c. 17.

(iv.) Pawnbrokers, subject in case of refusal to an appeal to quarter sessions.   1872, c. 93.

(v.) Passage brokers and emigrant runners.   1855, c. 119, ss. 66, 75.

(vi.) Gang masters of agricultural gangs (*b*).   1867, c. 130.

The justices in special or petty sessions have also other purely administrative duties, *e.g.*, appointing overseers, allowing rates, and revising jury lists.

NOTES.

Note (*a*). The present chapter only deals with justices' licenses, or what are called in some of the licensing acts "certificates." Excise licenses are also required in every case where intoxicating liquor is sold, except for beer sold under a billiard license, but these licenses are granted as a matter of course on the justices' license (when necessary) being obtained.   *Excise Licenses.*

Note (*b*). Besides the above, the following miscellaneous powers of regulating by local authorities may be here mentioned:—

(i.) Infant homes have to be registered by the local authority, *i.e.*, the council in a borough, and justices in petty sessions elsewhere.   *Infant homes.* 1872, c. 38.

(ii.) Pedlars, hawkers and chimney-sweepers employing apprentices are licensed by the police, but the justices in petty sessions hear appeals from refusal to grant pedlars' certificates.   *Pedlars, &c.* 1871, c. 96. 1861, c. 21, s. 6. 1875, c. 70.

(iii.) Justices (acting judicially) may order the registration of old metal dealers convicted of receiving stolen property.   *Metal dealers.* 1861, c. 110.

(iv.) Hackney carriages, horses for hire, and pleasure boats within any urban sanitary district may be licensed and regulated by the sanitary authority.   *Cabs, &c.* 1875, c. 55, ss. 171, 172.

(v.) Wherever a dog is found mad, the local authority may make orders as to the control of all dogs within their district. The local authority are the town council of a borough, the commissioners of an improvement act district and elsewhere the justices in petty sessions. The local rate is the police rate in all cases.   *Dogs.* 1871, c. 56.

(vi.) County justices in quarter sessions, and borough justices in special sessions may license retreats for habitual drunkards.   *Retreats.* 1879, c. 19.

CHAPTER XI.

LUNATICS.

(1) *Pauper Asylums.*
(2) *Private Asylums.*
(3) *Criminal Lunatics.*

(1) PAUPER ASYLUMS.
1838, c. 14.
1853, c. 97.
1855, c. 105.
1856, c. 87.
1862, c. 111.
1863, c. 110.
1865, c. 80.

THE areas for the purpose of the Lunatic Asylums Acts are (1) the "county" and (2) the "borough." Neither of these terms is used in its natural or ordinary sense (*a*) (*b*), and there are in fact very few boroughs which are separate lunacy areas. Subject to this qualification, the organization is as follows:—

In the "*county,*" a "Committee of Visitors," annually appointed by the justices in Quarter Sessions out of their own number, is the acting lunacy authority. In the "*borough,*" a "Committee of Visitors," annually appointed by the borough justices, is the acting lunacy authority; but the Council of the borough might, within six months after the Act of 1853, supersede the justices and appoint a "Committee of Visitors" from its own members. If any area has more asylums than one it must have a separate Committee for each, unless the Secretary of State allows one Committee to act for both. Every Committee has a paid clerk. The Committee either provides asylum accommodation, or contracts for accommodation in the asylum of some other authority or body, or unites with some other authority or body in the manner mentioned below. The Committee makes general rules for the government of its asylum, which must be approved by a Secretary of State, and they may make supplemental rules for minor matters. Every asylum must have its medical officer, clerk, treasurer, chaplain, &c., and provision is made for superannuations. The Committee reports to the Quarter Sessions and to the Lunacy Commissioners.

Expenses.
1853, ss. 95-102.
1861, c. 55, s. 6.
1862, s. 45.

The expenses in the "*county*" are defrayed out of (1) a weekly charge for each lunatic, which cannot, unless with the consent of a majority of all the justices, exceed 14*s*. a week (*c*), and which is charged (together with expenses of conveyance, burial, &c.) on the common fund of the union (or parish not in union) in which the lunatic is settled, or from which he is "irremovable," or if he is removable and he has no settlement, then on the "county" or "borough" where he was found; (2) a special county rate leviable over the whole "county," including places exempt from ordinary county rates, and excluding only boroughs with separate Quarter Sessions and recorders; and (3) contributions based on population from such of the last-mentioned excluded boroughs as are not themselves separate lunacy areas. The expenses in the "*borough*" are defrayed by a similar weekly charge and by the borough fund, or a special borough rate in the nature of a county rate.

Elaborate provision is made for the combination (or "union") of lunacy areas and authorities with each other or with private undertakers. The combined authorities appoint a joint Committee of Visitors, and the expenses are borne proportionally to the populations, or (if so agreed) to the estimated demands for accommodation. Combinations may be dissolved by the Joint Committee, with the assent of the Secretary of State. *Union of Areas.* 1853, 1855.

Besides the public lunatic asylums treated of above, there are asylums kept by private persons for the reception of both pauper and non-pauper patients. These are known as "licensed houses" or "registered hospitals," and are outside the immediate jurisdiction of the Lunacy Commissioners (see 1845, s. 14) licensed by the justices of a county in Quarter Sessions, and by the justices of a Quarter Sessions borough (with the consent of the recorder) in special sessions held at the same times as Quarter Sessions. Such justices are also required at their Michaelmas Sessions in every year to appoint three or more of their number and also a medical practitioner to act as visitors of every such "licensed house." (2) PRIVATE ASYLUMS. 1845, c. 100. 1853, c. 96. 1862, c. 111. 1876, c. 61, s. 26.

1845, ss. 114, 115.

The asylums for criminal lunatics are wholly under the control of the Secretary of State; but the expenses of their maintenance are to some extent charged on the common fund of the unions where the lunatics are settled (1864, s. 5). (3) CRIMINAL LUNATICS. 1840, c. 54. 1860, c. 75. 1864, c. 29. 1867, c. 12. 1869, c. 78.

All asylums are subject to visitation by the Commissioners of Lunacy (1845, s. 110).

NOTES.

Note (*a*). Each "county, riding, or division" is a county for the purposes of lunacy. Also the city of London is treated as a separate county, and also any county of a city, or county of a town, which has a separate court of Quarter Sessions and a clerk of the peace but no recorder. Haverfordwest seems to be the only place which is now within the last category. *County Areas.* 1853, c. 97, ss. 131, 132. 1862, s. 48. 1865, s. 1.

Every city or borough (except as above) not having a recorder, and also every liberty, is merged in ("annexed to *and treated and rated as part of*") the county by which it is surrounded, or if not surrounded by one county is merged in such one of the adjoining counties as may have been appointed under the repealed Act of 1845 (c. 126), or as the Secretary of State appoints. A borough or liberty so merged in a county for which an asylum was provided before the merger is liable, if it did not contribute towards building the asylum, to a charge towards paying off the cost of building the asylum. This charge is to be proportioned to population, and is to be paid out of a special rate apparently in the nature of a county rate.

It will be observed that a lunacy "county" may be different in area from the county for any other purpose.

Besides the boroughs and places which are merged as above described, most of the boroughs with recorders are "annexed," in a different sense, to counties as mentioned in the next note.

Borough Areas.
1849, c. 82.
1853, ss 8–10.
1855, s. 7.

Note (b). A borough with a separate court of Quarter Sessions and a recorder is *primâ facie* a separate lunacy area. But even such a borough is in any of three cases "annexed" to the county, namely :—

(i.) If in 1845 it had not six borough justices besides the recorder; or
(ii.) If it has made default in performing its duties as a lunacy area, and has therefore been annexed to the county by the Secretary of State; or
(iii.) If it is a borough constituted since 1853.

A Quarter Sessions borough which is so annexed appoints (by its recorder) two of its own justices to be members of the Committee of Visitors of the county, and it contributes to the lunacy expenditure of the county, according to population, out of its borough fund or out of a borough rate. Moreover, if a new asylum is provided for the county, each annexed Quarter Sessions borough appoints two members of the building committee.

Any Quarter Sessions borough which was annexed under the repealed Act of 1845 (c. 126), and continued so annexed in 1853, is empowered to separate itself (if it has the six justices) and to act as a separate lunacy area, and to cease to contribute to the county expenditure).

Cost of lunatics.
1862, ss. 6, 7.

Note (c). The ordinary weekly charge of 14s. for a lunatic may be increased in respect of cost of buildings where the county from which the lunatic is sent has not contributed towards erecting the buildings; and in that case the county from which he is sent may pay the whole or part of the extra charge (not exceeding one-fourth of the total charge) in relief of the parish to which the lunatic is chargeable.

CHAPTER XII.

SCHOOLS.

(1) *Elementary Schools.*
(2) *Poor-Law Schools.*
(3) *Reformatory and Industrial Schools.*

THE Elementary Education Act, 1870, was passed to ensure the proper provision of public elementary schools, and the efficient education of children at those schools. For this purpose, school-boards may be elected anywhere, and must be elected in any district where the amount of public school accommodation is found by the Education Department of the Privy Council to be insufficient. (1) ELEMENTARY SCHOOLS.
1870, c. 75.
1872, c. 27.
1873, c. 86.
1874, cc. 39, 90.
1876, c. 79.
1880, Sess. 2, c. 23.

For the election of School Boards under the Elementary Education Acts, the "school district" is ordinarily the Poor-law parish, but in municipal boroughs it is the borough. Where a parish is only partly included in a borough, the excluded part is treated as a distinct parish. The Education Department has power to unite school districts, and to merge small parishes in others, and to form "contributory districts." 1870, ss. 40-50.

The school authority is a School Board consisting of from 5 to 15 members, who hold office for three years. It is elected by ballot and the cumulative vote—in boroughs by the burgesses, and in parishes by the ratepayers. The duties of a School Board are to provide, maintain, and manage a sufficient number of public elementary schools. It is subject to the general control and inspection of, and may be dissolved by, the Education Department.

The Elementary Education Act, 1876, prohibits the employment of all children below the age of 10, and also of children below 14, if they have not either reached the standard of proficiency (No. 4) or made the number of attendances (250 for five years) prescribed by the Act. The prohibition is to be enforced (except in factories, &c.) by the School Board, or if there is none, then by a School Attendance Committee of the town council in a borough, or elsewhere of the guardians of the union in which the child's parish is included. These same authorities are, under the Acts of 1876 and 1880, to 1876, ss. 5, 48.

enforce the attendance at an elementary school of all children not otherwise educated, and to make bye-laws for regulating their attendance. In their default the Education Department may themselves make bye-laws, or may supersede a defaulting School Board or School Attendance Committee. In an urban district which is not a municipal borough, and which is co-extensive with a parish or parishes having no School Boards, and which has a population of not less than 5,000, a School Attendance Committee may, with the leave of the Education Department, be appointed by the Urban Sanitary Authority. In certain other cases members of the Local Board may be associated with the School Attendance Committee of the guardians (*a*).

<small>1870, s. 54.
1876, ss. 31, 33.</small>

The expenses of School Boards or School Attendance Committees (so far as they are not defrayed by Parliamentary grants, loans, or school fees) are to be paid in a borough out of the borough rate, in a parish out of the poor rate, and in a union or urban sanitary district out of a common fund raised by contributions from the several parishes as in the case of the common fund for the relief of the poor. In no case does a School Board levy its own rate.

<small>(2) POOR-LAW SCHOOLS.
1844, c. 101, ss. 40–49.
1848, c. 82.
1868, c. 122, ss. 10–12.</small>

Besides the ordinary work-house schools established under the Poor Law Amendment Acts, school districts for the education of pauper children, may be formed by the combination of unions and parishes not in union. These districts are formed and altered by order of the Local Government Board with the consent of the majority of the guardians in each union or parish. The authority of a school district is a district board composed of the chairmen of the boards of guardians and of qualified ratepayers elected by the guardians. The expenses of the schools are charged on the constituent unions and parishes in proportion to their rateable values. School districts are not common outside the metropolitan area. In 1883 there were only four so situated.

<small>(3) REFORMATORY AND INDUSTRIAL SCHOOLS.
1866, cc. 117, 118.
1872, c. 21.
1877, c. 21, s. 52.
1880, Sess. 2, c. 15.</small>

Reformatory and industrial schools may be provided either by any "prison authority" (*i.e.*, the County Quarter Sessions or the town council of a borough), or by any private persons. They must be inspected and may be certified by inspectors of prisons. A prison authority may contribute to a certified school of either kind, and must pay the cost of the conveyance and outfit of young persons committed to a certified reformatory school. The expenses incurred by a prison authority in respect of these schools are defrayed out of the county or borough rate. Guardians of a union may, with the consent of the Local Government Board, contribute towards the cost of children sent

<small>1870, c. 75, ss. 27, 28.
1876, c. 79, s.15.
1879, c. 48.</small>

to a certified industrial school on their application. School Boards may also contribute to or provide industrial schools; and where there is a School Board in a borough, the town council cease to have any powers in respect of industrial schools. Treasury subventions are given to certified schools of both kinds.

NOTE.

Note (*a*). (i.) Oxford is exceptionally treated by the Education Acts. The School Board is there elected for the Local Board district, and the rate is the General District Rate. Wenlock is also an exception, being treated as a parish, not as a borough.

(ii.) On April 1st, 1884, there were 142 School Boards in boroughs having an aggregate population of 7 millions, and 2,014 School Boards for 2,796 parishes, having an aggregate population of 5¼ millions.

(iii.) The School Board loans outstanding at Michaelmas, 1882, amounted to £11,841,000, including the Metropolis.

CHAPTER XIII.

BURIAL.

(1) *Parishes.*
(2) *Boroughs.*
(3) *Other Districts.*

THE common law appears to give to every person dying in a state of indigence, and not being "within certain exclusions laid down by the ecclesiastical law," a right to christian burial in the parish churchyard at the expense of the person under whose roof he dies. And it seems that before the Compulsory Church-Rate Abolition Act (1868, c. 109), it was lawful for a vestry, if they thought fit, to make a church-rate for the purposes of enlargement of the churchyard. The Church Building Acts and the Poor Relief Acts contain enabling enactments for the provision and enlargement of churchyards; and special Acts for the provision of cemeteries as commercial undertakings were common enough to render expedient the Cemeteries Clauses Act, 1847.

But the only systematic legislation for burials is contained in the recent series of acts, known as the "Burial Acts," which provide for the prohibition of burials within urban limits, the closing of overcrowded or insanitary burial grounds, and the appointment of burial boards. The first of these acts was passed in 1852, and was limited to the metropolis and its immediate neighbourhood, but in the next year it was made universal.

Under the Burial Acts the *area* is *primâ facie* the common law or civil parish, but may be almost any parochial or quasi-parochial area (*a*). The *authority* is a burial board of three to nine ratepayers elected by the vestry or select vestry, and the *rate* is the poor-rate. The adoption of the Acts is in general optional. It is practically compulsory where an Order in Council closes existing churchyards either on the ground of their condition, or on the ground that they are within a town. And when a board has been appointed, the board becomes practically independent of the vestry, for the board is empowered to fill up vacancies in itself on default by the vestry to elect; and it is also empowered, with the consent of a Secretary of State, to raise the

Marginalia:
See *R. v. Stewart,* 12 A. & E. 773.

In re St. John's, Cardiff, 16 L. J. M. C. 54.

Burial Acts.
1852, c. 85.
1853, c. 134.
1854, c. 87.
1855, c. 128.
1857 (2), c. 81.
1859, c. 1.
1860, c. 64.
1862, c. 100.
1871, c. 33.
1875, c. 55.
Sched.V.Pt.III.
(1) PARISHES.
R. v. Sudbury, E. B. & E. 264.

1855, ss. 5, 6.

necessary money for providing a burial ground or cemetery by mortgage of the rates without the authority of the vestry. The management of the cemetery is vested in the board, subject to regulations which may be made by a Secretary of State for the protection of health and decency, and subject, as regards inscriptions in consecrated grounds, to the discretion of the bishop. The fees for interment are fixed by the board with the assent of a Secretary of State, subject to limits prescribed by the Acts in the case of paupers. The board appoints a clerk and other officers. It may, instead of providing a cemetery of its own, contract for accommodation in the cemetery of some other authority or company. It may undertake the care of disused burial grounds (*b*). 1852, s. 44.
s. 38.
1855, s. 7.
1852, s. 49.
s. 25.
1855, s. 18.

Any parishes (whether common-law or poor-law) which have appointed boards may "concur" in providing a common burial-ground, and agree for the apportionment of expenses; and in that case their boards are to act as one board. Again, any parishes or places which in 1855 had been united for any ecclesiastical purpose, or had had a common church or burial-ground or a joint vestry for common purposes, may unite in appointing a joint board, and the expenses are to be apportioned according to the poor-law valuations; but the consent of a Secretary of State is necessary if either of the uniting parishes or places is a poor-law parish or has a separate burial-ground. *Union of Parishes.*
1852, s. 23.
1855, s. 11.
1857, s. 9.

By Order in Council made on the petition of the council of a municipal borough (after the compulsory closing of any burial-grounds of parishes wholly or partly within the borough), the council of the borough may be made the burial-board for all or any of the parishes wholly or partly included in the borough, and the powers of the vestries of such parishes are thereupon superseded; and the expenses are to be paid out of the borough fund or rate, unless any parish has been excepted on the ground that it is already sufficiently provided with a burial-ground, in which case the expenses of the borough-board must be paid out of a special separate burial rate assessed like a borough-rate on the area not so excepted. If the borough board acts for any part of a parish which is outside the borough (and, therefore, not liable to the borough or special rate), higher fees are to be charged for interment of persons from that part. (2) Boroughs.
1854, ss. 1–9.

By Order in Council made on the petition of any local board or improvement commissioners (after the compulsory closing of any burial-grounds within their district), the board or commissioners may be made the burial-board for their district; provided there is (3) Other Districts.
1857, s. 4.
1860, ss. 1–3.

not already a burial-board for the district, and provided that the district is not wholly included in or conterminous with one municipal borough. Their expenses are payable, at their option, out of the general district-rate (or improvement-rate), or out of a separate burial-rate on the same basis. It will be observed that under these enactments the burials area must be identical with the local government or Improvement Act district.

1875, c. 55, Sched. V. Part III.

By the Public Health Act, 1875, the burial-board for any area included in or conterminous with the district of any urban sanitary authority may, by agreement with the vestry and the urban authority, transfer all its powers, duties, &c., to that authority. By the same Act the vestry of any parish "comprised in a local government district" may constitute the "local board," or, if the parish forms a ward of the local government district, the ward members of the local board, the burial-board for the parish; and the expenses are payable out of a special general district-rate on the parish.

Sanitary Authorities. 1875, c. 55, s. 141. 1879, c. 31.

Besides the above-mentioned powers given to burials-boards proper, both urban and rural sanitary authorities may now provide cemeteries and mortuaries, and regulate their use by bye-laws, and acquire land for this purpose, and borrow with the consent of the Local Government Board. The expenses are paid as other sanitary expenses. These powers are now being extensively exercised.

Guardians. 1857, s. 6.

Guardians, with the consent of the Local Government Board, may appropriate land in their possession for a cemetery for paupers. The expenses are charged on the common fund. Relatives of the deceased persons may object to the burial in such cemeteries.

1847, c. 65.

There are also many cemeteries established under local Acts, usually incorporating the Cemeteries Clauses Act, 1847 (c).

NOTES.

Burial Areas.

Note (a). Although the common-law or civil parish is *primâ facie* the area for the purposes of the Burial Acts, these Acts may be adopted by various smaller or other districts, namely :—

    (i.) By any poor-law parish. (1852, s. 52.)
    (ii.) By any parish, township or district which is not a poor-law parish, but which before the Act of 1855 had a separate burial-ground. (1855, s. 12.)
    (iii.) By any "parish, new parish, township or other district" which is not a poor-law parish, and although it has not had a separate burial-ground (1857, s. 5), and this notwithstanding that there already exists a burial board for

the whole common-law parish in which the new area is included. (*Reg.* v. *Walcot*, 31 L. J., M. C. 221.)

(iv.) And if a portion of any area which could be a burial board district adopts the Acts, it follows that the remainder of the area may separately adopt them. (*Viner* v. *Tunbridge*, 28 L. J., M. C. 251.)

The only check upon the confusion which these provisions are calculated to produce is the enactment in sect. 4 of the Act of 1860, that where a parish or place is ecclesiastically divided, and any part of it has a separate burial-ground, the whole parish or place cannot adopt the Acts without the consent of a Secretary of State.

Wherever, under the provisions of the Burial Acts, a part only of a parish forms or is included in a burial board district, the burial board certify to the overseers the sums required from such part, and the overseers levy either a special poor-rate or additional pence with the ordinary poor-rate on such part. 1855, s. 13.

Note (*b*). There must be an unconsecrated part in every cemetery provided under the Burial Acts, with four exceptions, mentioned below. If there is a consecrated chapel there must also be an unconsecrated chapel, unless it is dispensed with by a Secretary of State on the application of three-fourths of a Vestry. In order to prevent encouragement of the use of the unconsecrated part, it is provided that equal fees must be taken in that part, less only the amount representing Ecclesiastical Fees. *Consecration, &c.* 1852, s. 30. 1853, s. 7. 1855, s. 14. 1857, s. 17.

The four exceptions above referred to are the following :—

(i.) Workhouse Cemeteries. These must be consecrated, and only Church of England rites can be used (1857, s. 6; but see 1880, Sess. 2, c. 41).

(ii.) Cemeteries provided under the Church Building Acts may, by agreement, be transferred to a Burial Board, with any debts incurred for them, and must be used as consecrated ground. But unconsecrated additions may be made to them (1857, s. 7).

(iii.) Any Burial Board may, with the consent of a Secretary of State, provide several cemeteries, and the consecrated and unconsecrated grounds may be distinct and separate (1857, s. 3).

(iv.) A Vestry, by unanimous vote, may resolve that a cemetery shall be in all respects a mere substitute for their former churchyard and similarly consecrated and used. But at any time within ten years from such resolution the Vestry may provide a separate unconsecrated ground (1855, s. 10).

No cemetery under the Burial Acts can be established within 100 yards of any dwelling-house, unless with the consent of the owner, lessee, and occupier. 1854, s. 12. 1855, s. 9.

Note (*c*). Besides the Acts mentioned above, there are the following miscellaneous provisions as to burial-grounds and burials :— *Miscellaneous.*

1285, c. 6 (*St. Win.*). Prohibition of fairs and markets in churchyards.

1285 (*Circumsp. ag.*). Enclosure of churchyards.

1808, c. 75. Burial of bodies cast on shore. Charge on county rate.

1816, c. 141. Ecclesiastical Corporations may sell land for cemeteries. Twenty years from consecration bars all adverse claims.

1846, c. 68. Single chapel for several burial grounds. (Amended 1851, c. 97, s. 28; and see 1855, s. 16.)

1850, c. 101, s. 2. Guardians, out of common fund, or parish, out of poor-rate, may contribute to provision or enlargement of consecrated burial ground of parish in which workhouse is situate, or of any parish in the same union, and on their so doing they acquire a right to bury paupers there from the workhouse.

1855, c. 79. Power to bury paupers in another parish, where the proper churchyard is closed or unfit.

1864, c. 97. Registration of burials. And see 1853, c. 134; and 1857, Sess. 2, c. 81, ss. 15, 16.

1867, c. 135. Fees on consecration, &c.

1869, c. 26. Simplification of title to burial grounds of religious bodies.

1880 (2), c. 41. Right of parishioner to be buried in churchyard or graveyard without Church of England service.

CHAPTER XIV.

DRAINAGE AND EMBANKMENT.

GENERAL powers for regulating drainage and defence against water are given to local authorities by three classes of Acts ; namely—

(1.) The Sewers Commissions Acts ;
(2.) The Land Drainage Act, 1861 ; and
(3.) The Public Health Act, 1875.

In addition to these general powers there are many local Acts, and in some places (as Romney Marsh) there are ancient laws of " sewers," which do not derive their authority from any known Acts of Parliament.

There are also Acts giving large powers to owners for the improvement of their lands by drainage, including compulsory powers over the lands of other persons to be exercised with the sanction of the Inclosure (now the Land) Commissioners. 1847, c. 38.
1864, c. 114, s. 33.
1877, c. 31.

The following is a summary of the provisions of the three classes of general Acts above mentioned :—

The Sewers Commissions Acts provide for the appointment (under the great seal) of Courts of Commissioners of Sewers for districts which may include the whole or any parts of a county or counties. Their jurisdiction extends only to the sea coast and navigable or tidal rivers, or such watercourses as "shall or may directly or indirectly communicate" with navigable or tidal rivers. Their powers include the supervision, erection and maintenance of sea and river walls and of sluices, and the scouring of watercourses and other means of defence against the sea, and of relief from superfluous land waters. Each court may divide its district into sub-districts, and may levy general or special sewers rates, either throughout their district or in distinct levels or sub-districts. By the Act of 1841 (s. 1), the assessment of a rate on lands in each parish or place within a district is to be so made, " that such lands and hereditaments shall contribute thereto in proportion to the benefit and advantage received or capable to be received from the said court, as compared with the lands and hereditaments of the other parishes, townships, or places within such jurisdiction." The principal officers or (1) *Sewers Commissions Acts.*
1531, c. 5.
1533, c. 10.
1549, c. 8.
1571, c. 9.
1708, c. 33.
1833, c. 22.
1841, c. 45.
1849, c. 50.

servants of a Sewers Court are a clerk, a treasurer, a surveyor and dyke reeves. It has compulsory powers for taking land.

The powers of these Commissions for the purposes mentioned in the Acts are limited by two restrictions. Firstly, they cannot act (except in emergency) unless upon a presentment made by a jury. Secondly, by the Act of 1833 (s. 21), no new works can be made without the consent of three-fourths in value of all the owners and occupiers in the "valley, level, or district" proposed to be charged with the cost.

By the Act of 1841, the sewers rates are to be assessed in gross on each parish, township, or place, in proportion to the benefit received by each of these areas; and the sum payable by each area is to be further apportioned among the occupiers in that area.

(2) *Land Drainage Act,* 1861, c. 133.

The Land Drainage Act, 1861 (which followed upon a number of Acts for encouraging drainage by individual owners), extends to inland as well as maritime places. It provides in the alternative for two kinds of organization, namely:—

    a. Drainage "areas," under new Commissions of Sewers;
    b. Drainage "districts," under elective drainage boards.

The areas or districts may be of any extent.

The powers which these bodies may exercise are *primâ facie* of the most extensive kind, including the construction or maintenance of every kind of work for defence of land against water, or for relieving land from water, and including unlimited powers of rating. But these *primâ facie* powers are subject to important limitations.

    a. As regards "Commissions of Sewers for Drainage Areas," the Act is limited as follows:—

- (i.) The jurisdiction of an old Commission of Sewers cannot be affected without the consent of that Commission (s. 4);
- (ii.) A petition for a new Commission shall be dismissed if one-third of the proprietors in the proposed area dissent (s. 5);
- (iii.) No mill-dam, weir, or other like obstruction can be interfered with, if two justices in petty sessions determine that the injury "is not of a nature to be fully compensated for by money" (s. 17);
- (iv.) No land can be taken compulsorily, except by Provisional Order, confirmed by Parliament (s. 21);
- (v.) Improvements or works costing more than £1,000 cannot be made if the owners of half the land which is to be rated for them dissent (s. 31);
- (vi.) The Commissioners cannot interfere, except by consent, with any sewers or drainage works, made under any local Act, or with canals, waterworks, &c., worked for profit, or under local Acts (ss. 54, 57).

b. Elective drainage boards for "separate drainage districts" must be constituted by Provisional Order, confirmed by Parliament, and made on the motion of the owners of one-tenth of the land affected, and with the approval of the owners of two-thirds of the land. No place within the limits of any Commission of Sewers or of any urban sanitary district can be included in a "separate drainage district" under this Act without the consent of the Commissioners of Sewers or urban sanitary authority.

Whenever any works under this Act involve an expenditure exceeding £1,000, the expense is to be defrayed out of a rate levied on owners exclusively. In other cases the rate is apparently to be levied as under the old Sewers Commissions Acts (s. 38).

Under the Public Health Act, 1875, both urban and rural sanitary authorities are sewer authorities within their districts. In this Act "sewer" includes any sewer or drain, except such as are private or under the control of a distinct highway authority, and except sewers made and used for irrigation, or made and used under local Acts for improvement of land, and except sewers under Commissions. The sanitary authority have the following powers with respect to sewerage as distinguished from sewage. They may buy sewers within their district, make, maintain and alter sewers, and carry them through roads, &c. They may also connect with the sewers or (for purposes of outfall) traverse the roads of an adjoining sanitary authority, by its consent or with the sanction of the Local Government Board, and an owner or occupier outside the district may communicate with their sewers. Moreover, united districts with a joint board may (apparently on the application of any one district) be constituted by Provisional Order for this as for any other special sanitary purpose; or even without a Provisional Order the sanitary authorities of adjoining districts may combine for common works, or each such authority may permit the execution of works in its district by the other.

(3) *Public Health Act,* 1875, c. 55, ss. 13—34.

ss. 279—285.

Expenses of sewerage under this Act are *primâ facie* chargeable on the general district rate in urban districts, or in rural districts on the poor rate, but with the same three-fourths exemption of agricultural land, railways, canals, &c., as the general district rate.

ss. 210, 229.

It must often happen that the effectual exercise of the powers of the Act will be defeated by the very large provisions of ss. 327 and 332, prohibiting sanitary authorities from interfering with private water-rights of the various kinds mentioned in those sections.

(See generally for suggestions for Water-shed Boards a paper by Lord R. Montague, Parliamentary Papers $\frac{18\,7\,6}{3\,1\,3}$).

CHAPTER XV.

VALUATION AND LOCAL ACCOUNTS.

(1) *Valuation.*
(2) *Audit of Local Accounts.*
(3) *Local Taxation Returns.*

(1.) VALUA-
TION.
1601, c. 2.
1744, c. 38.
1801, c. 23.
1836, c. 96.
1848, c. 110, s. 7.
1862, c. 103.
1864, c. 39.
1868, c. 122.
1869, c. 41, s. 13.
1874, c. 54.
1880 (2), c. 7.

IN this and the following chapter it is proposed to give a brief review of the most important matters incident to local finance, excluding rates, which have been already dealt with in previous chapters. (See especially pp. 22, 30.)

Of these perhaps the most important is the settlement of the valuation list for poor law purposes, since that list is conclusive for the great majority of local rates, *i.e.*, for the poor rate and all those levied on the basis of the poor rate, including borough and urban sanitary rates, and also (by the Highway Assessment Act of 1882, c. 27) for highway rates (*a*).

1862, 1864, 1880.

1862, s. 45.
1880, s. 2.

1836.

The following is an outline of the ordinary mode of valuation under the Union Assessment Acts, 1862 to 1880, which apply to all parishes in a union formed under the Poor Law Amendment Acts, and may also be applied by order of the Local Government Board to other parishes, whether under separate Boards of Guardians or in union under any local Act. In separate parishes not under the Union Assessment Acts, or a local Act (*b*), there is no valuation list properly so called, but the "assessment" (see Ch. VI. p. 26) is made by the overseers, and is subject to appeal to the justices in Special Sessions. In these cases, however, a general survey and valuation of property rateable in the parish may be made at any time on application of the overseers by order of the Local Government Board.

Rateable value.
1836, s. 1.

The Valuation list of a parish is a statement of the rental and rateable value of all the rateable property in the parish. By the Parochial Assessment Act of 1836, every poor-rate must be made "upon an estimate of the net annual value of the several hereditaments rated thereunto; that is to say, of the rent at which the same might reasonably be expected to let from year to year, free of all usual tenants' rates and taxes, and tithe commutation rent-charge, if any, *and deducting therefrom the probable average annual cost of the repairs, insurances and other expenses, if any, necessary to maintain them in a state to command such rent:* Provided always, that nothing herein contained shall be construed to alter or affect the principles or different relative liabilities (if any), according to which different kinds of hereditaments are now by law rateable." By the Act of 1862, s. 15, every valuation must also show the "gross estimated rental," which is to be calculated in the same way, but without the deductions shown in *italics* above.

The settlement of the valuation list of a parish includes three stages, viz. :— *Settlement of valuation list.*

(i.) The preparation of a list by the overseers of the parish.
(ii.) The correction of the list by the Assessment Committee of the guardians of the union.
(iii.) Appeals to the justices in Special Sessions, Quarter Sessions and the Superior Court.

It will be convenient to describe at the outset the constitution of the Assessment Committee under the Act of 1862.

The guardians of every union formed under the Act of 1834 must annually appoint an Assessment Committee out of their own members. The number may be from six to twelve. One-third must be ex-officio guardians if so many exist. The appointment is made in April or May. If the union is conterminous with a municipal borough, the council of the borough may, on the invitation of the guardians, appoint an equal or less number of councillors to be members of the Committee.

The overseers in every parish prepare a list, which is ordinarily a copy of the last approved valuation list, with such alterations (if any) as the overseers think proper to make. This list is deposited in the parish for inspection during fourteen days, and notice of the deposit is published. It is then transmitted to the Committee.

Within twenty-eight days from the notice of deposits (or in certain cases at any time, see 1868, s. 1), any aggrieved person or parish may give notice of objection to the Committee and to parishes or persons affected by the objection. The objection must be on the ground of unfairness, incorrectness or omission in the valuation. The Committee hear and determine the objections. They may also, with or without objection, and at any time and on any information, make such alterations as they think fit, and they may employ a person to value generally or in any special case. When satisfied they approve and sign the list. If they have altered it, it is re-deposited, and it may come back to them for a fresh hearing and approval. Also if any alteration is made necessary by the decisions of Special Sessions or Quarter Sessions (see below), the Committee alter the list accordingly. Finally, they add up the totals of gross rental and of rateable value, and approve and sign the list and deliver a copy of it to the overseers, and they also send the parish totals of gross rental and rateable value to the clerk of the peace. The list as so approved and delivered becomes "the valuation list in force," subject to supplemental lists which may from time to time be made and approved in

F

Appeals.

like manner. The valuation list, as so settled, becomes the only legal basis for the poor-rate and for any other rate leviable on the basis of the poor-rate; and the contributions of the several parishes to the common fund of the union are calculated according to the totals of their rateable values in this list, with the addition of any Government contribution in respect of Government property in a parish. Guardians may appoint a permanent salaried valuer to assist the Committee.

Appeals either against a valuation list or against a rate made in conformity with a valuation list must be made in the first instance by objection before the Assessment Committee. A person aggrieved by anything relating to valuation (as distinguished from liability to be rated) may appeal from the Committee to the Justices in Special Sessions, and from them to the Quarter Sessions. A person alleging that he is not liable to be rated at all must (and he may on any other ground, except perhaps the amount of his valuation) appeal directly to the Quarter Sessions. A parish may by its overseers, with the consent of the vestry, appeal directly to the Quarter Sessions against an alleged over-valuation in its own case or under-valuation in the case of any other parish, and the Quarter Sessions may alter the lists and may order a re-valuation, and may order the union or the appealing parish to pay the costs. In any case in which appeal lies to the Quarter Sessions on a matter of law (not of amount), a case for the opinion of a Superior Court may be obtained. Notice of any appeal to Special Sessions or to Quarter Sessions must be given to the overseers and to the Committee, who may appear as respondents.

The process of re-valuing a parish or union as now generally conducted is too expensive to be annually repeated. The correction of valuations is commonly left to supplemental lists, which are seldom thorough. But a great portion of the country has within the last few years been completely revalued (*c*).

(2.) AUDIT OF LOCAL ACCOUNTS.
(Poor Law &c).
1844, c. 101, ss. 32, 49.
1852, c. 81, s. 33.
1868, c. 109, s. 3.
(School Boards).
1870, c. 75, s. 60.
(Highways).
1878, c. 77, s. 9.
(Sanitary).
1875, c. 55, ss. 247, 248.
(General).
1879, c. 6.
(Boroughs).
1875, c. 55, s. 26.

THE accounts of unions and poor-law parishes, of school-boards, highway authorities, and (with the exception of boroughs where the council are the sanitary authority) of sanitary authorities, are audited by district auditors appointed by the Local Government Board. The overseers' accounts in respect of the county rate, and churchwardens' accounts (where the church rate is still compulsory) are similarly audited. District auditors are now in all cases paid by salary, and a stamp duty proportioned to the total expenditure audited is levied on the local rate (1879, s. 3). A district auditor has full powers of disallowance, surcharging, compelling the production of all necessary documents, &c., and any person aggrieved by his certificate may appeal to the Local Government Board, or move for a writ of *certiorari*.

In boroughs the municipal accounts (and also where the council are the sanitary authority, the sanitary accounts) are audited half-yearly by three auditors. One of these is a councillor appointed by the mayor, and the other two are elected yearly by the burgesses. The elective auditors must be qualified to be, but must not be, councillors. These borough auditors are not ordinarily paid, but are entitled to certain fees for auditing sanitary accounts. They have no express powers of disallowance. 1882, c. 50, ss. 25—27, 62.

In counties the treasurers' accounts are audited by the justices in Quarter Sessions. 1852, c. 81, s. 50.

In parishes adopting the Select Vestry Act, 1831, auditors are chosen out of the persons qualified to be vestrymen to audit and approve all the parish accounts. 1831, c. 60, s. 32.

The accounts of parochial burial boards are audited yearly by two auditors appointed by the vestry. 1852, c. 85, s. 18.

ANNUAL returns of all compulsory rates, taxes, tolls, or dues (other than such as are levied for the public revenue of the United Kingdom), and of the expenditure thereof, are to be made by the clerk, treasurer, &c. of every local authority (including the town clerk of a borough) to the Local Government Board, and an abstract of them is to be laid before Parliament. The returns are to be made up to the end of the financial year (25th March), and are to be sent in within one month of that date, or of the completion of the audit. The returns of school boards and some minor authorities are, however, made up to Michaelmas and other different dates. (3.) LOCAL TAXATION RETURNS.
1860, c. 51.
1871, c. 70.
1877, c. 66.
1879, c. 39.
1882, c. 50, s. 28.

NOTES.

Note (a). Besides the valuation for the poor rate, there are (outside the metropolis) separate and independent valuations for county and other (e.g., sewers) rates, and for property tax. The county rate is assessed by the justices, but only on whole parishes. The property tax is assessed by the Assessors, Surveyors, and Commissioners under the Income-tax Acts (see Ch. III., p. 14, Appendix, p. 115). *County, &c., valuations.*

Note (b). It must be observed that there are still a number of places which, by reason of the existence of local Acts, are or were excepted from the operation of the Union Assessment Committee Act, 1862. In 1874 they were of the net rateable value of £16,000,000, and included Liverpool, Manchester and Birmingham. *Local Acts.*

Note (c). A comparison of the more complete system of valuation now in force in the metropolis is appended:— *Valuation in Metropolis.*

The Valuation (Metropolis) Act, 1869, differs from the Union Assessment Committee Act of 1862 in the following principal respects:— 1869, c. 67.

    1. The overseers are to send a copy of their lists to the surveyor of taxes, who sends his corrections to the Assessment Committee (s. 8), and his figures are to be inserted unless proved wrong (s. 53), and he may appeal (ss. 18, 32).

2. The overseers are to give notice to occupiers of alterations in their valuations (s. 9).
3. A Special Court of Assessment Sessions is substituted for the Quarter Sessions as the court of appeal from the ordinary Special Sessions (ss. 23, &c.).
4. Any Assessment Committee or body levying rates or contributions from the metropolis or county may appeal against any valuation list for any parish (s. 32).
5. A valuation lasts for five years, but provision is made for an annual revision and for the insertion of new buildings (ss. 43-7).
6. The approved list is made conclusive as regards valuation for nearly all rates and taxes, and for juror and other qualifications under various Acts of Parliament (s. 45).
7. A maximum scale of deductions from gross rental is laid down (s. 52).
8. Owners and occupiers may be required to make returns of values, charges, &c., under a penalty, in the same way as for income tax (ss. 55-58).

The practical effect of this improved system of valuation is shown by comparing the income-tax and poor-rate (gross rental) valuations in recent years inside and outside the metropolis. These were in 1880 almost identical in the metropolitan unions, while elsewhere the poor-rate fell short of the income-tax valuation by 10·5 per cent. on the average, and in some counties by as much as 20 or 30 per cent. For the necessity for a new Valuation Act outside the Metropolis, see the remarks of Sir J. Lambert before the H. of L. S. C. on Highways, 1881 (p. 822).

CHAPTER XVI.

LOCAL LOANS.

MOST of the loans of local authorities are raised on the security of the rates levied by them. But under the Municipal Corporations and certain other Acts, sums may be borrowed on the security of land and other property belonging to the authority. And loans raised under local Acts for gas, water, market, harbour and the like undertakings by a rating authority are usually charged on the revenues of the undertaking, with the rates as a collateral security in case of deficiency. And see the Public Works Loans Act, 1882, for a general power enabling the Board of Trade, with the sanction of the Local Government Board, to authorize an urban sanitary authority to charge the rates as security for a loan raised by a public body for harbour purposes in the same place. *1882, c. 50, s. 106. 1875, c. 36, s. 22. 1875, c. 55, s. 235. 1882, c. 62, s. 7.*

Local authorities cannot borrow on the security of the rates without the sanction of Parliament, which may be given either by special or general Acts. *Modes of borrowing.*

Borrowing powers conferred on local authorities may be exercised in various ways. They may borrow in the open market either in the mode prescribed by the Act conferring the powers, or under the provisions of the Local Loans Act, 1875, and either with or without the sanction of the Treasury, Local Government Board, or other Government department. They may also borrow in certain cases from the Government itself through the Public Works Loans Commissioners. Each of these modes is treated of shortly below.

A. Borrowing under a special Act without Government control. *Special Acts.*

This is the method of borrowing most in favour, especially with large corporations. Borrowing powers to an amount considerably exceeding £33,200,000 have been conferred by Parliament on sanitary authorities alone during the ten years 1873–82. Many of these Acts allow a long period for repayment, 60 to 100 years being not uncommon.

B. Borrowing under the Local Loans Act, 1875. *Local Loans Act. 1875, c. 83.*

This Act does not itself confer any borrowing powers. It merely suggests certain advantageous modes in which borrowing powers given by other Acts of Parliament may be exercised, and authorizes the use of those modes. A local authority, having Parliamentary borrowing powers, may, if it pleases, exercise them in one of the modes provided by this Act, notwithstanding that a different mode may have been prescribed by an old special Act which gave the powers.

The principal advantages of adopting the Act are :—

(i.) That inconvenient forms of mortgage deeds, &c. prescribed by old special Acts may be avoided.

(ii.) That if the local authority obtains the sanction of the Local Government Board after investigation of its financial position (s. 26), its securities cannot be impeached for informality or want of power to issue them. These latter provisions have not, however, been taken much advantage of, less than £800,000 in all having been raised with official sanction during the five years 1877-82.

Government sanction.

1882, c. 50, s. 106.
1873, c. 86, s. 10.
1875, c. 55, s. 233.
1852, c. 85, s. 20.

C. Borrowing with the sanction of a Government Department. This is the mode prescribed by the Municipal Corporations, Elementary Education, Public Health (as regards rates), Burial, and other Acts. The sanctioning Department varies with the class of authority. Very large sums are yearly raised with this sanction, *e.g.* by sanitary authorities alone with the sanction of the Local Government Board no less than £25,900,000 in the ten years 1873-82.

Public Works Loans Commissioners.
1875, c. 89.
1876, c. 31.
1878, c. 18.
1879, c. 77.
1882, c. 62.

D. Borrowing from the Public Works Loans Commissioners under the provisions of the Public Works Loans Act of 1875 and amending Acts.

These Commissioners are empowered at their discretion to advance money to local authorities for any of the following purposes mentioned in the schedule to the Act of 1875 :—

Baths and wash-houses provided by local authorities.

Burial grounds provided by burial boards.

Conservation or improvement of rivers or main drainage.

Docks, harbours and piers, or "any other shipping purpose."

Improvement of towns.

Labourers' dwellings.

Lighthouses, floating and other lights for the guidance of ships, buoys and beacons.

Lunatic asylums of any county or borough.

Police stations and justices' rooms of any county or borough.

Public libraries and museums.

Any school-house or work for which a school board is authorized to borrow under the Elementary Education Acts.

Waterworks established or carried on by a sanitary or other local authority.

Workhouses and any work for which guardians of the poor are authorized to borrow under the general Acts relating to the relief of the poor.

Any work for which a sanitary authority are authorized to borrow under the Public Health Act, 1875.

The Commissioners may also lend for the purposes of the Artisans' Dwellings Acts and the Contagious Diseases (Animals) Act, and for borough buildings authorized by the Municipal Corporations Act. 1875, c. 36, s. 22, &c. 1878, c. 74, s. 49. 1882, c. 50, s. 120.

In exercising their discretion as to granting a loan the Commissioners "shall have regard to the sufficiency of the security for its repayment, and, subject to the provisions of any special Act, shall determine whether the work for which the loan is asked would be such a benefit to the public as to justify a loan out of public money, having regard to the amount of money placed at their disposal by Parliament." 1875, c. 89, s. 9.

Interest is to be paid at not less than 5 per cent., or, where a lower rate is authorized by the special Act, at a rate to be fixed by the Treasury (1879, s. 2). The principal is to be repaid by instalments, within not more than 20 years, unless where a special Act prescribes some other limit.

Besides many local Acts the following general Acts grant specially favourable terms for loans. Under the Public Health and the Artisans and Labourers' Dwellings Acts, 1875, the rate of interest may be 3½ per cent., or such rate as will prevent loss to the Exchequer, if the loans are recommended by the Local Government Board. Loans under the Public Health Act are, however, only made at this lower rate for strictly *sanitary* purposes. Under the Elementary Education Acts the recommendation of the Education Department is necessary, and the rate of interest is to be 3½ per cent. A similar rate is prescribed for loans under the Harbours and Passing Tolls Act, 1861, except when the aggregate amount is less than £100,000, when the rate is to be only 3¼ per cent. Each of the above Acts also authorizes an extension of the period for repayment to 50 years. Now, however, under the Act of 1879 the Treasury have full power to raise all special statutory rates to an amount sufficient to prevent loss to the Exchequer, and to vary the amount according to the length of term for repayment. 1861, c. 47.

The security for the loan (except where a special Act otherwise prescribes) must include— 1875, ss. 12—16.

    a. Mortgage of property or of a rate, or of both, and also,
    b. Unless specially dispensed with, personal security in addition to the mortgage.

Advances cannot be made except out of moneys specially provided by Act of Parliament for Public Works Loans in each year. In the case of loans granted after the passing of the Act of 1879 not more than £100,000 can be advanced to any one borrower in any one year. 1879, s. 3.

Where a loan is granted on the security of a rate, the Local Government 1875, s. 36.

1878, s. 4. Board are to see that it is duly applied, and may order any sum misapplied to be replaced out of a local rate.

A history of the former Public Works Loans Commissioners will be found in the first report of the new Commissioners ($\frac{1876}{209}$). The accounts appended to their last report ($\frac{1883}{209}$), show that, down to 31st March, 1883, about 50½ millions have been advanced in Great Britain and Ireland since the year 1817, besides more than 3 millions advanced on accounts which are finally closed. £1,610,000 of this 3 millions has been remitted or is irrecoverable, the principal remission being that of £1,370,000 for Irish workhouses. About 22 millions of principal have been repaid, and 28 millions are outstanding. It appears that during the three years, 1880-1882, sums amounting to £5,768,000 (£1,920,000 a year) have been lent by the Commissioners, at rates varying (according to the term for repayment) from 3¼ to 5 per cent., and averaging 3⅞ to 4 per cent. These sums were advanced by the National Debt Commissioners at 3½ per cent.

PART II.

AMOUNT OF LOCAL TAXATION AND INDEBTEDNESS.

A.—*General Remarks.*

The principal sources of revenue of local authorities are the poor rate, the county rate, the borough rate, the general district rate, and the highway rate. All of these, except the general district rate, and except rates for special sanitary expenditure in rural places, are levied uniformly on all descriptions of real property. There is no limit of amount, except in the case of highway rates (which are limited to 2s. 6d. in the pound), and some minor rates for special purposes. *[Principal rates.]*

There are difficulties, amounting to impossibility, in the way of ascertaining with any accuracy from the published returns either the present total amount of local taxation and expenditure, or the comparative amounts in urban and rural districts, or even the actual amount in any year of purely urban expenditure in urban places, or the rate at which the burden of local taxation as a whole has increased and is increasing. *[Difficulties in statistics.]*

Firstly: The total present amount cannot be ascertained, because all the returns are much in arrear, and because the returns of different authorities are not made up to the same date. The Annual Local Taxation Returns, published in January, 1884, give the poor law, highway, sanitary, county, and borough returns down to Lady Day, 1882, but the school-board accounts are only brought down to Michaelmas, 1881, and those of sewer, drainage and some other minor authorities end at various dates between 31st of May, 1881, and 1st of June, 1882. The last report of the Local Government Board, published in June, 1883, is for the year 1880–1, *i. e.*, for most purposes it stops with March, 1881.

Secondly: It is impracticable to compare, except conjecturally, the expenditure in rural and urban districts. Unions and parishes cross the boundaries of boroughs and local board districts, and it nowhere appears, and it would probably be impossible, in the present state of local government, to ascertain, with any approximation to accuracy, what share of poor relief falls on urban and what on rural places. Of the county expenditure, again, it is not known how much falls on boroughs, how much on local board districts, and how much on rural places. So of the school-rate, as between local board districts and rural parishes, which are partly included in them.

Thirdly: Even within urban sanitary districts, and taking into consideration merely urban sanitary purposes, the elements for an accurate statement of ordinary expenditure and taxation are not given. The capital expenditure on sewerage, on streets, on gas-works, and on water supply, is not distinguished from the ordinary expenses of maintenance and supply, and no complete distinction is made between places which supply their own gas and water and those in which these are supplied by private enterprise.

There are many other points in respect of which caution is necessary in the use of the published returns. For instance, those returns do not show accurately the amount of the Treasury subvention actually given for any particular purpose in each year, and thus leave obscure the effect which such contributions have had on the growth of local burdens. Again, the importance of an apparent increase in rural highway expenditure is much qualified, when it is remembered that the rapid abolition of turnpikes has transformed into rates a large sum formerly paid in the shape of tolls.

<small>Simplification of areas necessary.</small>

Some of the defects which have been referred to could probably have been made good in former returns, and can be cured in future ones. But no care in abstracting the accounts of *twenty-four* distinct kinds of local authorities, differently constituted, having different but often overlapping and interlacing areas, using different periods of account, and levying separate rates or contributions on different bases and valuations, could possibly elaborate a clear budget of local finance. It is certain that the effects of this confusion are more than mere statistical perplexity, and that it has an important tendency to perpetuate extravagance and waste. Practically the only way of proving that affairs are too expensively administered in any particular place is to show that similar affairs are less expensively managed in other places on an average or under similar circumstances; and this cannot, in the present state of things, be shown (unless by accident) with regard to some of the most important parts of local administration. Even if no other good result were likely to follow from a simplification of areas and authorities, the value of such simplification as a necessary condition for comparison of expenditure and taxation can hardly be overrated.

Subject to the foregoing remarks, the Tables appended to this Part illustrate some of the most important points with regard to the amount and growth of local taxation and indebtedness. *Remarks on Tables.*

Table A. includes the Metropolis, and shows for the whole of England and Wales the rateable value, receipts, expenditure, and debts for 6 out of the last 15 years; omitting only the receipts, expenditure and debts on account of some matters which are of the nature of property rather than of expenditure, such as market and harbour tolls, dues, &c. The general result may be stated in the form of a comparison between the years 1867-8 and 1881-2, as follows (in millions) :—

	1867–68.	1881–82.	Increase per cent.
Rateable value (apparent increase (¹))	100¾	139¼	38·7
Receipts of all kinds, including new loans (²)	25	51¼	105·3
Ditto, excluding new loans	20½	38⅓	86·4
Expenditure of all kinds, including capital account (which cannot be distinguished)	25	50½ (³)	101·7
Debts outstanding at the end of the year	33	120¾	263·8

NOTES.—(¹). The apparent increase in rateable value is in great part merely the effect of recent re-valuations. A large number of unions had not, until lately, been re-valued for many years.

(²). It would have been desirable to exclude the capital expenditure as well as the new loans; but as the amount of the former is not shown separately, it is necessary for comparison to include both.

(³). Of this expenditure 11⅜ millions was for repayment of and interest on loans.

Tables B. and C. are more instructive. They distinguish between—

Part I. Boroughs and local boards, urban purposes only (*Metropolis excluded*);

Part II. Rural places, rural purposes only (*Metropolis excluded*);

Part III. Poor rates, School Board rates, &c., which are common to both urban and rural places (*Metropolis included*).

Part I. shows at a glance the enormous increase (from 16½ to 76 millions) in urban debts during the years from 1868 to 1882. It will also be observed that at the end of 1881-2 the borough and urban sanitary debts were nearly equal to a year and a half's rateable value of the boroughs and other urban districts, and that the annual charge of those debts was to the municipal and sanitary rates as 29 to 35.

Part II. shows that the rural debts, though far smaller in proportion than the urban, have been increasing equally steadily. Rural sanitary debts, which did not begin to be incurred until about 1873, had risen to £1,218,000 in 1881-2.

From Part III. it appears that there has been a further rise of some 17 millions in undistinguishable urban and rural debts. But of this increase it is satisfactory to note that nearly 12 millions are due to the operation of school boards, and not more than $3\frac{3}{4}$ millions have been borrowed for unremunerative poor-law purposes. Of the 17 millions increase, at least 5 millions have been incurred in the Metropolis.

Table D. shows the new borrowing powers granted to urban authorities (*Metropolis excluded*) since 1871. Probably these powers have been exercised to a large amount since 1881-2, and the urban debts shown in the preceding tables will have increased accordingly. Assuming this net increase to be one-third of the amount authorized, the urban debts at the commencement of 1884 may be taken as nearly £80,000,000, and the annual charge for them (including instalments and sinking fund) at one-tenth of this, or £8,000,000, which is equal to 2s. 10d. in the £ on the whole rateable value.

Table E. contains a list of all the boroughs and shows the number of urban districts, which at the end of 1881-2 owed more than one year's rateable value. No less than 94 boroughs and 107 other urban districts are in this unsatisfactory position. It must further be remembered that, if Poor Law, School Board, and other debts (which cannot, owing to the overlapping of areas, be included in the Table) were added, not a few other places could be shown to be in the same category.

A debt of one year's rateable value may be taken on an average as involving at the present time an annual charge of about 2s. in the £ in urban places. Where the loans are for long periods, the charge is less in proportion, and wherever the loans are new, the annual charge is less in proportion to the debt outstanding. As the principal of a debt is diminished, the instalments remaining the same, the annual charge necessarily bears a larger proportion to the amount of the debt remaining. Thus, during the years 1876-9 the ratio of annual charge to the total debt actually diminished, but this did not mean any improvement in the financial position, but merely an increase in the amount of new loans, or in the periods allowed for repayment, or in both. The ordinary period for repayment of loans was formerly from 30 to 50 years (see the Return, "County and Borough Loans," $\frac{487}{391}$), but the periods allowed by recent local Acts are longer, ranging from 40 to 60 years, and in some cases to 80 and 100 years, usually with some additional years of grace, before the repayment commences. However, since the passing of the Public Works Loans Act, 1879, which in effect enabled the Commissioners to raise the rate of interest for long loans under special Acts (see Ch. XVI. p. 71), both the length of the periods for repayment and the ratios of increase in the debts have somewhat diminished, and the ratio of charge to debt has correspondingly been increasing. This is shown in Table C.

It has not been unusual in late years, where an urban authority has applied to Parliament for new borrowing powers, for it also to apply for and obtain an extension of the periods prescribed by former local Acts for the repayment of old loans.

Table F. shows the urban sanitary expenditure for three years under each of the heads shown in the Local Taxation Abstract (*Metropolis excluded*).

Table G. is an analysis of local expenditure in 1881-2 (*excluding the Metropolis*), according to the several purposes for which it was incurred, and **Table H.** shows the amounts of each class of expenditure repaid to the local authorities by the Treasury.

It appears to be useless to attempt to estimate the average amount of local taxation in urban and rural districts respectively. Firstly, there are no materials for ascertaining the cost in the £ of poor relief in urban as compared with rural districts. Secondly, the urban districts vary so much as compared with each other, and the rural districts vary so much as compared with each other, that an average of either would be merely misleading. Thirdly, there are no materials for ascertaining what is really the amount of ordinary urban expenditure, because the ordinary expenditure for gas and water supply and other "sanitary" purposes is not distinguished from the capital expenditure.

In the consideration of the question, how far the debts are likely to go on increasing out of proportion to the means of the localities, it is necessary to remember that under the Public Health Act, 1875, loans to the extent of two years' rateable value can be incurred for the purposes of that Act alone without any resort to Parliament. If to

1875, c. 55, s. 234.

this possible amount of now about 225 millions (*excluding the Metropolis*) there is added the amount of the loans likely to be authorized by local Acts of Parliament, and the amounts which may be required for schools—to say nothing of the debts existing or which may be required for purposes of workhouses, county and borough buildings, &c.—the total of indebtedness may assume very grave proportions before its importance is fully realized.

Growing importance of the subject.

In conclusion, the growing importance of local finance may perhaps be best realized by comparing (i.) the increase in the amount of rates levied by local authorities in England and Wales, with (ii.) the increase in the amount of Imperial taxation chargeable to England and Wales during the same years. The following Table shows these items at three different periods, ending with the latest year for which reliable returns of both can be obtained. To complete the comparison, the amounts contributed in each year out of the taxes for local purposes in aid of the rates are also shown.

Year.	Total amount of Local Rates (excluding Tolls, Dues, and Rents).	Total amount of Taxation (excluding Post Office and Miscellaneous Receipts).	Government Contributions for Local purposes. (excluding Rates on Government property).
	£	£	£
1867—68	16,430,000	48,570,000	951,000
1875—76	22,593,000	50,408,000	1,918,000
1879—80	25,694,000	53,223,000	2,732,000

It thus appears that while the burden on the taxpayer only increased by 9·6 per cent. in the twelve years, that on the ratepayer increased by 56·4 per cent., while the amount levied on the taxpayer, and applied in aid of the ratepayer, increased by 187·3 per cent.

B.—TABLES OF LOCAL TAXATION.

TABLE A.

COMPARATIVE STATEMENT FOR THE WHOLE OF ENGLAND AND WALES (*including the Metropolis*) IN EACH OF THE YEARS 1867-8, 1873-4, 1875-6, 1879-80, 1880-1 AND 1881-2 OF THE FOLLOWING PARTICULARS:—

i. Rateable Value.
ii. Receipts of Local Authorities (other than tolls, dues and rents).
iii. Government Contributions towards the expenditure of Local Authorities.
iv. Expenditure of Local Authorities (other than on account of tolls, dues and rents).
v. Local Loans outstanding (other than loans on tolls, dues and rents).

Note 1.—This Table does not include the receipts, expenditure, and loans of those authorities whose revenue is derived entirely from tolls, dues, rents, or other sources in the nature of revenue from property. It includes only authorities levying rates for the purpose of local expenditure. The following accounts are accordingly excluded:—Pilotage, Turnpikes, Harbours, Markets and Fairs, Bridges and Ferries, Mercantile Marine Fund, and also the accounts of the City of London, except as regards the Police, Sewers, and Ward Rates.

Note 2.—Compiled from the following publications :—

Report of Mr. Goschen M.P., on local taxation ($\frac{1870}{470}$).
The Annual Local Taxation Abstracts.
The Statistical Abstract for the United Kingdom.
The Annual Reports of the Local Government Board.
The Annual Reports of the Committee of Council on Education.
The Annual Accounts of the Chamberlain of the City of London.
The Annual Accounts of the Metropolitan Board of Works.
The County Treasurers' Accounts for 1873-4, and 1875-6.
The Municipal Borough Rates Accounts for 1873-4, and 1875-6.
The Annual Accounts of Highway Boards.

Note 3.—In the earlier years (before the Act of 1877, c. 66) the accounts of the various authorities were made up to very different dates. The accounts of most of the authorities are now made up to March 25th in each year. The principal exceptions are the accounts of the Metropolitan Board of Works, made up to December 31st, and the School Board accounts, made up to 29th September. In no case, however, is more than 12 months' receipts and expenditure included.

Year.	Rateable Value assessed to the Poor Rate.	RECEIPTS.			EXPENDITURE.		Loans outstanding at the end of the Financial Year.
		Sources of Receipt.		Total.	Total.	Amount for Repayment of Loans and Interest thereon, included in previous Column.	
	£		£	£	£	£	£
1867—68 (a)	100,669,000	Rates Government Contributions Loans Other Sources	16,430,000 951,000 (b) 4,449,000 3,208,000	25,038,000	25,002,000	Cannot be given.	33,180,000 (c)
1873—74	115,647,000	Rates Government Contributions Loans Other Sources	19,773,000 1,001,000 6,687,000 (d) 4,672,000	32,133,000 (d)	31,318,000	4,415,000	59,647,000
1875—76	121,833,000 (e)	Rates Government Contributions Loans Other Sources	22,593,000 1,918,000 8,741,000 (f) 4,961,000	38,213,000	37,759,000	6,107,000	70,826,000 (g)
1879—80	133,770,000	Rates Government Contributions Loans Other Sources	25,694,000 2,732,000 (h) 12,165,000 7,047,000	47,638,000	46,872,000	8,634,000	107,042,000 (i)
1880—81	135,645,000	Rates Government Contributions Loans Other Sources	26,819,000 2,706,000 (k) 11,461,000 7,209,000	48,195,000	48,383,000	9,515,000	113,934,000 (l)
1881—82	139,636,000	Rates Government Contributions Loans Other Sources	27,891,000 2,841,000 (m) 13,019,000 (n) 7,649,000	51,400,000	50,418,000 (o)	11,627,000	120,721,000 (p)

OBSERVATIONS.

(*a.*)—The figures for 1867-8 are taken from Mr. Goschen's tables, with some necessary corrections. The returns on which these are based end at various dates during the years 1867-9.

(*b.*)—Partly estimated.

(*c.*)—This is the amount of loans outstanding at the end of 1868-9. No earlier information can be given, and to a certain extent even this must be considered as approximate.

(*d.*)—Exclusive of loans raised by poor-law authorities during the year. These may be estimated at from £450,000 to £500,000.

(*e.*)—Estimated.

(*f.*)—The actual amount raised on loan by poor-law authorities during the year is not stated—the sum authorized by the Local Government Board for poor-law purposes has therefore been included, viz., £589,000.

(*g.*)—Of this amount £38,500,000 was the debt of urban sanitary authorities.

(*h.*)—Includes £514,000 Government grants to School Boards. Besides these contributions the Government had in 1878 taken over the county and borough prisons, a transfer which relieved the county and borough rates of an annual expenditure of about £400,000.

(*i.*)—The debts of urban sanitary authorities amounted to 61¼ millions, over 50 millions being for boroughs. The School Board debts had almost reached the sum of £10,000,000.

(*k.*)—Includes £625,000 Government grants to School Boards.

(*l.*)—Urban sanitary debts were in this year further increased by 4½ millions. School Board debts amounted to nearly 11 millions, and the debts of municipal boroughs to nearly 6½ millions.

(*m.*)—For the items of contribution, see Table H., p. 92.

(*n.*)—6¼ millions of this was raised by borough urban sanitary authorities.

(*o.*)—For an analysis of this expenditure, see Table G., p. 89. The accounts do not distinguish between capital and ordinary expenditure.

(*p.*)—Urban sanitary debts had reached 69 millions, 55¼ being for borough authorities. Poor-law loans outstanding were 5½ millions; debts of municipal boroughs over 6¾ millions, Metropolitan Board of Works over 16¼ millions, and School Boards nearly 12 millions.

TABLE B.

COMPARATIVE STATEMENT OF THE GROWTH OF RATES AND DEBT IN EACH OF THE YEARS MENTIONED IN TABLE A (EXCLUDING THE METROPOLIS FROM PARTS I. AND II.), DISTINGUISHING URBAN AND RURAL PURPOSES. COMPILED FROM THE RETURNS MENTIONED IN TABLE A.

PART I.—URBAN AUTHORITIES FOR URBAN AREAS AND PURPOSES, VIZ., MUNICIPAL BOROUGHS AND OTHER URBAN SANITARY AREAS ; AND COMPRISING THE BOROUGH RATES, BOROUGH POLICE RATES, AND URBAN SANITARY RATES.

Years.	Rateable Value	Receipts from Rates.	Loans raised in the Year.	Loans repaid with interest during the Year.	Debt outstanding at the end of the Year.	Observations.
		£				(a) For the year 1868-69, see note to Table A.
1867—68	{ Municipal Boroughs { Other Urban Districts	} Not stated.	3,008,000	1,685,000	Cannot be given.	16,580,000 (a)	
1873—74	{ Municipal Boroughs { Other Urban Districts	24,500,000 14,300,000	5,317,000	3,507,000	2,362,000	35,115,000	(b) The Rates for Water and Gas supply in Boroughs and Districts where these are supplied by the Sanitary Authorities, and the Gas and Water Loans, are included in all the years. In 1881-2 the gas and water receipts (exclusive of private rates) amounted to £2,915,000, and the expenditure to £3,674,000. See Table F. (p. 88).
1875—76	{ Municipal Boroughs { Other Urban Districts	25,713,000 19,068,000	8,106,000	5,877,000	4,175,000	44,304,000	
1879—80	{ Municipal Boroughs { Other Urban Districts	32,618,000 20,276,000	9,383,000	7,560,000	5,817,000	67,864,000	
1880—81	{ Municipal Boroughs { Other Urban Districts	33,752,000 21,300,000	10,270,000	7,992,000	6,788,000	72,527,000	(c) It will be observed that in 1882 for the first time the charge for loans exceeds the new loans raised. Some 3 millions of the charge, however, were for interest.
1881—82	{ Municipal Boroughs { Other Urban Districts	34,831,000 20,618,000	10,508,000 (b)	8,606,000	8,659,000 (c)	75,995,000	

LOCAL TAXATION AND INDEBTEDNESS.

PART II.—RURAL AUTHORITIES FOR RURAL AREAS AND PURPOSES, AND COMPRISING THE FOLLOWING RATES, VIZ., COUNTY RATES, COUNTY POLICE RATES, RURAL HIGHWAY RATES, AND RURAL SANITARY RATES.

Years.	Rateable Value of Rural Sanitary Districts.	Receipts from Rates.	Loans outstanding at end of the Year.	OBSERVATIONS.
	£	£	£	(a) County Rates are partly levied and expended in or for Urban Areas. Rural Sanitary Rates (including about £101,000 for highway purposes) amounted to 332,000l. in 1881-82. Rates levied for highway purposes increased from £1,378,000 in 1867-68 to £1,922,000 in 1881-82. (b) Rural Sanitary Debts increased from about 100,000l. in 1873-74 to 1,218,000l. in 1881-82.
1867—68	Cannot be given.	2,879,000	2,694,000	
1873—74	53,191,000	3,519,000	3,153,000	
1875—76	56,709,000	3,417,000	3,392,000	
1879—80	57,308,000	3,611,000	3,823,000	
1880—81	56,866,000	3,547,000	4,123,000	
1881—82	56,661,000	3,744,000 (a)	4,372,000 (b)	

PART III.—MIXED OR UNDISTINGUISHABLE PURPOSES (POOR LAW; SCHOOL BOARDS; BURIAL BOARDS; DRAINAGE, SEWERS, AND EMBANKMENT COMMISSIONS; CHURCH RATES, &c.).

N.B.—*The Metropolis and Urban and Rural places are all included in this Part, except in so far as regards the Metropolitan Board of Works, Metropolitan Police, and City of London Accounts, which being entirely peculiar to the Metropolis are excluded.*

Years.	Receipts from Rates.	Debt outstanding at end of the Year.	OBSERVATIONS.
	£	£	(a) Of these rates, 2,047,000l. (1,973,000l. Poor Law, and 661,000l. School Board), were levied in the Metropolis alone. (b) The increase in the debt outstanding is mainly on account of School Boards. The School Board Debts in 1873—74 amounted to less than 2,500,000l.; in 1879—80 they had increased to nearly 10,000,000l., and in 1881-82 to 11,899,000l. Of the last amount 4¼ millions were incurred in the Metropolis, and 3½ in municipal boroughs. The debt of Poor Law Authorities also increased from 1,786,000l. in 1867-68, to 5,561,000l. in 1881-82, at least a million of this increase being due to the Metropolis.
1867—68	8,225,000	4,100,000	
1873—74	8,711,000	8,561,000	
1875—76	8,716,000	10,427,000	
1879—80	9,708,000	18,288,000	
1880—81	9,990,000	19,622,000	
1881—82	10,889,000 (a)	21,073,000 (b)	

TABLE C.

STATEMENT SHOWING, WITH RESPECT TO PART I. OF TABLE B, THE INCREASE PER CENT. IN THE RATEABLE VALUE OF URBAN AREAS, AND IN THE RATES, DEBTS, AND CHARGE FOR DEBTS OF URBAN AUTHORITIES IN EACH YEAR, SINCE 1873–4, FOR WHICH THE PARTICULARS ARE STATED IN TABLE B.

	Rateable Value.	Rates.	Charge for Debts.	Amount of Debts Outstanding.
	Per Cent.	Per Cent.	Per Cent.	Per Cent.
Increase in 1875–6 over 1873–4 .	14·8	52·5	63·0	26·2
Annual average . .	7·4	26·2	31·5	13·1
Increase in 1879–80 over 1875–6 .	18·1	18·2	39·3	53·2
Annual average . .	4·5	4·55	9·8	13·3
Increase in 1880–81 over 1879–80	4·1	7·1	16·7	6·9
1881–82 over 1880–81	0·7	2·3	27·6	4·8
Increase in 1881–82 over 1873–4 .	42·2	97·6	238·0	116·4
Annual average . .	5·3	12·2	29·75	14·55

TABLE D.

New Borrowing Powers granted to Urban Authorities (excluding the Metropolis) since 1871.

Years.	New Borrowing Powers given or sanctioned by the Local Government Board in each year, in respect of Sanitary Improvements.	Borrowing Powers granted by Parliament by Local Acts (exclusive of Powers required to be exercised only with the sanction of the Local Government Board).*
	£	£
1872	602,000	2,572,000
1873	959,000	1,347,000
1874	1,338,000	866,000
1875	1,836,000	6,236,000
1876	2,064,000	3,211,000
1877	3,080,000	4,142,000
1878	2,790,000	2,108,000
1879	2,871,000	6,418,000
1880	2,689,000	4,934,000
1881	2,265,000	1,548,000
1882	2,226,000	2,384,000
Total . . £	22,720,000	35,766,000
Grand Total .	£58,486,000	

* *Note.*—The figures given in this column are exclusive of all sums authorized to be borrowed by the issue of perpetual annuities, and also of sums borrowed under general powers conferred by Local Acts to borrow unascertained amounts for the purchase of particular undertakings.

TABLE E.

LIST OF BOROUGHS IN WHICH THE OUTSTANDING LOANS AT THE END OF THE FINANCIAL YEAR 1881-82 AMOUNTED TO MORE THAN ONE YEAR'S RATEABLE VALUE.

Note.—The Municipal and Urban Sanitary Debts are both included in this Table, as are also the School Board Debts in cases (marked *) of Boroughs having separate School Boards.

1. *Boroughs which owed three or more years' Rateable Value.*

Boroughs.		Rateable Value, 1882. £	Amount of Debt, 1882. £
Batley*	} 5 to 6 years. {	89,539	513,752
Huddersfield*		285,847	1,539,552
Birmingham*		1,520,197	7,082,548
Bradford*		922,456	3,962,185
Dewsbury*		115,868	482,595
Halifax*	4 to 5 years.	280,773	1,306,011
Leicester*		400,000	1,609,402
Stockton-on-Tees*		137,681	603,488
Barnsley*		88,500	266,278
Bolton*		394,534	1,433,469
Lancaster		71,955	238,718
Leeds*		1,131,593	4,198,170
Middlesborough*	3 to 4 years.	211,298	696,550
Penzance		36,577	110,496
Rochdale*		322,344	1,145,977
Wakefield*		142,540	464,230
Wigan		140,991	559,474

2. *Boroughs which owed between two and three years' Rateable Value.*

Boroughs.	Rateable Value, 1882. £	Amount of Debt, 1882. £
Aberavon	10,523	27,139
Aberystwith*	24,930	59,354
Ashton-under-Lyme	133,445	334,524
Barrow-in-Furness*	212,217	446,946
Birkenhead	403,579	907,744
Blackburn*	321,356	814,735
Burnley	142,786	306,078
Bury	224,008	644,588
Chorley	60,958	127,850
Darlington*	154,985	354,910
Doncaster	99,050	245,277
Lincoln	88,709	232,442
Longton*	58,112	159,863
Macclesfield	91,945	190,492
Manchester*	2,761,469	6,882,277
Nottingham*	737,648	1,893,826
Oldham*	510,582	1,071,876
Penryn	7,078	15,814
Peterborough	88,384	190,142
Preston	291,010	690,172
Reading*	159,645	384,067
Rotherham*	133,068	288,377
Southport	203,862	472,761
Stafford	53,063	153,948
Staleybridge	88,334	201,996
Swansea*	233,116	601,765
Warrington	139,480	282,223
Wolverhampton*	246,610	683,420

TABLE E.—(continued.)

3. *Boroughs which owed between one and two years' Rateable Value.*

Boroughs.	Rateable Value, 1882.	Amount of Debt, 1882.
	£	£
Abingdon	16,546	30,059
Basingstoke	29,242	42,750
Beaumaris*	9,066	10,739
Berwick-on-Tweed	62,700	65,199
Bideford*	15,398	26,552
Blackpool	104,710	174,392
Brecon*	22,121	22,518
Bridgwater*	36,163	46,719
Brighton*	659,612	691,021
Burslem*	96,110	175,227
Cardiff*	393,787	704,382
Carnarvon	27,146	45,580
Chesterfield*	42,112	50,272
Chichester	27,986	35,160
Colchester	99,852	132,445
Congleton	31,947	48,470
Dartmouth*	16,945	23,467
Derby*	339,030	590,315
Droitwich	18,727	35,852
Exeter*	187,888	247,403
Hereford	85,230	117,782
Heywood	100,708	148,853
Hythe	17,457	32,184
Ipswich*	182,252	189,617
Kidderminster*	71,494	133,534
King's Lynn	63,645	86,949
Kingston-on-Hull*	592,635	618,624
Liverpool*	3,422,949	5,053,301
Margate*	81,062	137,699
Newcastle-on-Tyne*	730,233	815,709
Newcastle-under-Lyme*	49,558	57,324
Norwich*	261,489	325,421
Over Darwen	88,829	177,334
Plymouth*	191,870	203,897
Retford, East*	40,188	53,490
Ripon	33,248	35,692
Ryde*	74,062	124,979
St. Helens	225,093	397,206
Salford*	799,618	1,581,542
Sheffield*	978,178	1,016,335
Southampton*	227,963	229,343
Stoke-on-Trent*	64,737	113,355
Stratford-on-Avon	31,606	45,410
Tamworth*	11,048	16,671
Tenby	19,048	25,624
Walsall*	112,748	162,905
Warwick	48,017	53,488
Wisbeach*	36,904	44,536
Yeovil*	26,579	37,686

Note.—It thus appears that in 1882, out of about 240 Boroughs 94 owed more than one year's rateable value. Of the other Urban Sanitary Districts, 10 owed more than three years', 16 others more than two years', and 81 others more than one year's rateable value (exclusive of School Board Debts). It must be remembered that a very large proportion of these debts (but it nowhere appears how much of them) is for remunerative works of water and gas supply. Another portion (equally uncertain, but not large) is secured on tolls or dues, and is remunerative as enabling those tolls and dues to be earned.

TABLE F.

COMPARATIVE STATEMENT OF THE RECEIPTS AND EXPENDITURE OF URBAN SANITARY AUTHORITIES IN EACH OF THE YEARS 1879-80, 1880-81, AND 1881-82. (METROPOLIS EXCLUDED.)

A.—RECEIPTS.

Sources of Receipt.	1879—80.	1880—81.	1881—82.
	£	£	£
Public Rates:—			
General and Special Rates	4,137,000	4,468,000	4,665,000
Highway Rate	396,000	474,000	377,000
Water and Gas Supply Rate	2,593,000	2,766,000	2,915,000
Private Rates (Improvement Rate and Water Supply Rate or Rent)	1,216,000	1,213,000	1,143,000
Market Tolls or other Dues	332,000	348,000	345,000
Parliamentary Grant in Aid of Medical Officers' and Inspectors of Nuisances' Salaries	23,000	23,000	24,000
Loans raised during the year	6,969,000	7,355,000	7,932,000
All other Sources of Income	2,792,000	3,137,000	3,518,000
Total Receipts . . . £	18,458,000	19,784,000	20,919,000

B.—EXPENDITURE.

Branches of Expenditure.	1879—80.	1880—81.	1881—82.
	£	£	£
Public Works:—			
Sewerage	884,000	635,000	585,000
Water Supply	1,578,000	1,714,000	1,256,000
Gas Supply	2,473,000	2,603,000	2,418,000
Highways, Scavenging, & Watering	2,428,000	2,346,000	2,655,000
Other Public Works	2,064,000	1,994,000	1,780,000
Private Improvement Works	508,000	431,000	835,000
Loans repaid with Interest and Sinking Funds	5,154,000	6,042,000	7,973,000
Salaries and Poundage	639,000	675,000	730,000
All other Charges	1,187,000	1,409,000	1,588,000
	16,915,000	17,849,000	19,820,000*
Add Loans of Urban Sanitary Authorities (other than Town Councils) raised during the year—the expenditure therefrom not being shown in the accounts	1,681,000	1,772,000	1,361,000
Total . . . £	18,596,000	19,621,000	21,181,000

* *Note.*—Of the Expenditure for the year 1881—2, shown above, £16,480,000 was incurred in Boroughs, and £3,340,000 in other Urban Sanitary Districts. The charge for debt amounted to £7,024,000 in Boroughs, and £949,000 in other districts.

TABLE G.

ANALYSIS OF EXPENDITURE FOR LOCAL GOVERNMENT PURPOSES IN THE YEARS 1874-75 AND 1881-82, EXCLUSIVE OF THE METROPOLIS.

	1874-75. £	1881-82. £
1. By *Poor-Law Guardians*: (¹)		
a. In relief of the poor—		
In-maintenance	1,111,000	1,262,000
Out-relief	2,682,000	2,428,000
Lunatics	690,000	837,000
Salaries, &c.	745,000	820,000
Workhouse loans repaid	171,000	206,000
Other expenses connected with relief	501,000	589,000
Total for relief of the poor . £	5,900,000	6,142,000
b. Not for Poor-relief (exclusive of valuation, registration, and vaccination expenses)	300,000	533,000
Add expenditure by County and Borough Authorities on account of Lunatic Asylums	414,000	425,000
Total . . £	6,614,000	7,100,000
2. By *County and Borough Authorities for Police, Reformatories, Prosecutions.* &c. :		
Police, counties	938,000	1,084,000
,, boroughs	649,000	824,000
Prisons, Reformatories, &c. (²)	385,000(²)	54,000
Prosecutions and maintenance of prisoners, counties	126,000	119,000
Ditto do. boroughs	57,000	73,000
Total . . . £	2,155,000	2,154,000
3. By *Highway and County Authorities for Rural Roads:*		
Parish highways	571,000	704,000
District highways (including South Wales)	990,000	1,147,000
Paid in aid of turnpikes (³)	43,000	18,000
Total . . . £	1,604,000	1,869,000

LOCAL GOVERNMENT.

TABLE G.—*continued.*

	1874-75. £	1881-82. £
4. *Sanitary Expenses and Public Works:* (⁴)		
a. By Borough Authorities—		
Public works, maintenance and repairs	937,000	735,000(⁵)
b. By Urban Sanitary Authorities (including Town Councils acting as Urban Sanitary Authorities)—		
Sewerage	583,000	585,000
Gas	1,502,000	2,418,000
Water	1,391,000	1,256,000
Streets	1,727,000	2,654,000
All other Public Works	1,380,000	1,781,000
Private Improvement Works	335,000	836,000
Repayment of loans, interest, and Sinking Fund	3,530,000	7,973,000
All other purposes (including salaries)	892,000	2,318,000
c. By Rural Sanitary Authorities—		
General expenses (including repayment of loans with interest)	144,000	510,000(⁶)
Special expenses	43,000	79,000
d. By Port Sanitary Authorities—		
Total expenditure	3,000	6,000
e. Lighting and Watching Act—		
Total expenditure	44,000	38,000
f. Burial Boards—		
Total expenditure (including repayment of loans with interest)	347,000(⁷)	414,000(⁷)
Total £	12,858,000	21,603,000
5. *School Boards:*		
Capital charges—building, furnishing, &c.	858,000	619,000
Maintenance of Elementary Schools		1,319,000
Other expenses (including repayment of loans with interest)	357,000	617,000
Total £	1,215,000	2,555,000(⁸)
6. *Miscellaneous:*		
County salaries	155,000	309,000
Borough ,,	192,000	266,000
County loan charges	411,000	388,000
Borough ,,	390,000	687,000
Valuation expenses (poor rate)	57,000	67,000
Vaccination fees ,,	72,000	81,000
Registration of births and deaths	72,000	79,000
Ditto of voters and juries	70,000	94,000
All other expenses, boroughs	535,000	728,000
Ditto counties	292,000	389,000
Drainage, Sewers, and Embankment Commissioners	203,000	443,000
From Church rates	17,000	6,000
Total £	2,556,000	3,537,000

TABLE G.—continued.

Summary of Expenditure:	1874-75. £	1881-82. £
Poor-relief, lunatics, &c.	6,614,000	7,100,000
Police, prosecutions, &c.	2,155,000	2,154,000
Rural roads	1,604,000	1,869,000
Sanitary and Public Works	12,858,000	21,603,000
School Boards	1,215,000	2,555,000
Miscellaneous	2,556,000	3,537,000
Total £	27,002,000	38,818,000[8]

THE TOTAL EXPENDITURE SHOWN IN TABLE A, FOR THE YEAR 1881-82, IS £50,418,000, A DIFFERENCE (DEDUCTING PAYMENTS IN AID OF TURNPIKES) OF £11,618,000. THIS DIFFERENCE IS ACCOUNTED FOR AS FOLLOWS:—

	£
Poor Law loans raised in the year (expenditure therefrom not being shown in accounts)	514,000
Urban Sanitary Authorities' loans (ditto)	1,361,000
	£1,875,000
Metropolis Poor-relief	2,278,000
,, Police	1,238,000
,, Local Management	2,144,000
,, Board of Works	2,390,000
,, Burial Boards	42,000
,, School Board expenditure	1,284,000
,, Church rates (expenditure from)	7,000
City of London, on account of sewers, police, and ward rates	360,000
Total £	11,618,000

[1] Exclusive of expenditure out of Poor Law loans raised during the year.

[2] All prisons were transferred by the local authorities to the Prison Commissioners in 1878.

[3] The total expenditure of turnpike trusts was £632,000 in 1874, and about £174,000 in 1881.

[4] The expenditure out of new loans raised in the year 1881-82 by Urban Sanitary Authorities other than Town Councils is not shown here. See Table F. Neither the returns for 1874 or 1881 distinguish between new works and maintenance.

[5] The decrease in municipal public works is only apparent, part of their cost being in 1881-82 included in the urban sanitary expenditure.

[6] Of this £85,000 was highway expenditure, and £190,000 was expended out of loans for sewerage and waterworks.

[7] These items include the amounts received as burial fees, £81,000 in 1874, and £150,000 in 1881.

[8] This is the total expenditure of School Boards, including expenditure out of parliamentary grants, school fees, &c. The amount of School Board rates levied in the year 1881-82 (exclusive of the Metropolis) was £1,111,000, while the parliamentary grants amounted to £521,000 and the school fees, &c., to £337,000.

[9] From the expenditure shown here must be deducted the amounts repaid by Government contributions shown in Table H.

TABLE II.

ANALYSIS OF GOVERNMENT CONTRIBUTIONS TO LOCAL GOVERNMENT PURPOSES IN THE YEAR 1881-82 (METROPOLIS INCLUDED).

	£
1. Poor Law, Lunatics, &c.:	
To Poor Law Guardians	537,196
To County and Borough Authorities for Lunatic Asylums	16,711
2. Police Prosecutions, &c.:	
To County Police	419,397
To Borough Police	351,843
To Metropolitan Police	585,482
For Criminal Prosecutions and Maintenance and Removal of Prisoners	159,339
3. Sanitary Purposes:	
For Salaries of Medical Officers and Inspectors	65,649
4. School Boards:	
Education Grant	695,407
5. Miscellaneous:	
Metropolitan Fire Brigade	10,000
Total	**£2,841,024**

Notes.—Since 1882 there has been a new item of subvention, grants amounting to about £165,000 being made towards the cost of maintenance of disturnpiked roads.

In addition to the Contributions mentioned in the Table, about £162,000 was paid in lieu of rates on Government property.

PART III.

CONSIDERATIONS WITH A VIEW TO AMENDMENT OF LOCAL GOVERNMENT.

A. *Areas.*

LEGISLATION for local affairs has proceeded by piecemeal, creating special districts and authorities for special purposes, instead of establishing units for general purposes of local government with one consolidated authority in each unit.

The result may be shortly illustrated as follows:—The inhabitant of a borough lives in a four-fold area for purposes of local government, namely, in the borough, in a parish, in a union, and in a county; none of these are conterminous (unless by accident) with any of the others; and different parts of the borough are or may be in different parishes and in different unions and in different counties. He is or may be governed by a six-fold authority, the council, the vestry, the burial board, the school board, the guardians, and the county quarter sessions: all these are different bodies; and inhabitants of different parts of the same borough are or may be under different vestries, burial boards, guardians, and county quarter sessions. He is or may be subject to a borough-rate, a general district-rate, a poor-rate, a burial-rate, and a county-rate. *[marginal note: Complexity and inconvenience of areas.]*

The inhabitant of a local board district also lives in four kinds of districts,—the local board district, the parish, the union and the county. He also is or may be under six governments,—the local board, the vestry, the union, the burial board, the quarter sessions and the school board. And any of these districts or authorities, except the local board and its district, may be different for inhabitants of different parts of the same local board district.

The inhabitant of a rural parish lives in a parish, in a union, probably in a highway district, and in a county. He is or may be governed by a vestry, a school board, a burial board, a highway board, the guardians, and the justices.

There are a multitude of minor matters in respect of which the districts, authorities, and rates are or may be additionally multiplied and complicated in all the above cases.

Lastly, whether in the borough, in the local board district, or in the rural parish, the inhabitant is or may be subject to a number of separate debts charged on the different areas which happen to include his house; and another inhabitant of the same place may be subject to a partly different set of debts charged on other areas and incurred by other authorities.

A second kind of accusation brought with justice against the existing system of local government is, that even disregarding the complexity which has been described, and looking singly at the area authority and rate existing for any one purpose, the area is often ill-arranged or too small or too large, the authority is not constituted in the best possible way, and the rate is unfair in its incidence.

It is said, and it seems to be beyond question, that by reason of the defects which have been described the machinery of local government works with waste and difficulty and without its proper effect; that some of the most capable men are deterred from taking their proper part in it; that by reason of the unfairness of taxation private interests are unnecessarily aroused against public improvements; and that local indebtedness is so broken up and is incurred under so divided a responsibility that its growth, which can only be checked locally, is not known locally, and could not be effectively resisted even if it were known.

Simplification necessary.

The statement of these defects in itself implies a statement of the direction in which amendment should proceed. So far as may be, local affairs ought to be administered in simple areas or aggregations of simple areas, without crossing or interlacing. "The unit of area should be the same for all local purposes, and larger areas should be as far as possible exact multiples or aggregates of that unit."* So far as may be, the local affairs of each area or aggregate of areas ought to be administered by one body for that area or aggregate. So far as may be, the rates should be unified in each area, and the debt of each area should be consolidated and ascertained. And the areas ought to be made of a convenient size, and the incidence of expenses ought to be made as equitable as is possible.

* Report of Sanitary Commission, 1871, vol. i. p. 54.

In devising a plan for securing these advantages certain limiting conditions have to be taken into account. *Firstly*, the least possible disturbance of existing arrangements and interests, and the greatest degree of utilization of existing institutions, which are compatible with securing the main objects, are not only desirable but necessary. *Secondly*, in determining what kind of area ought to be chosen as the unit for local government, it must be borne in mind that the class or body of purposes which are called "sanitary purposes" are at present, and are likely for a long time to continue to be (at least in urban districts), the dominant purposes of local government; and if those purposes can be best administered in areas of certain dimensions or of a particular character, it will probably be necessary or best to adopt such areas so far as may be for other purposes of local government, even though for some of these other purposes, if regarded alone, different areas might be preferable.

Bearing these considerations in mind, the question to be first answered is, what primary area or unit shall be adopted. As regards at any rate the larger boroughs and the larger local board districts, no radical change of area is to be thought of. As regards rural places, the choice appears to lie between the parish, the union or rural sanitary district, or some other area to be newly invented. The last of these is opposed to the principle of least disturbance of existing things, and could be adopted only in the last resort. The others are now to be compared. *Choice of primary areas.*

The Parish was proposed by Mr. Goschen in his Bill of 1871 as the primary unit of local administration in rural places. *Parish.*

Considerations in favour of adopting the parish are—(i.) that it is in most cases an ancient institution invested with a considerable amount of valuable local sentiment, which not only will be lost as an advantage if the parish is not made the ordinary unit, but also will operate as an impediment to the establishment of any other unit; and (ii.) that the parish comparatively seldom overlaps the county boundary, and has already been generally used as the foundation of unions and petty sessional divisions.

On the other hand, there are several considerations against accumulating upon the parish all the weight of primary local administration. The great inequality in population would necessitate an amount of grouping in the case of the smaller parishes, and of subdivision in the case of the larger ones, which would go far to destroy the value of the first of the considerations in its favour; and a further disturbance of the existing parish would have to be made in those numerous cases where the parish is cut by the boundary of a borough or other urban district. The vestries must be generally reorganized, and new officers must be appointed. The existing organization of unions and highway boards must be dissolved. And there are some purposes (as, for instance, indoor poor relief, highways and sanitary inspection) for which experience has conclusively shown a much larger area than the ordinary parish area to be necessary. Nor would it generally be possible to obtain from a population limited as that of the ordinary parish a sufficient number of persons qualified and willing to administer the local affairs.

Union.

The other alternative seems to be the Union, or such part of it as not being included in any urban area forms the existing rural sanitary district. The unions perhaps do not start with any popular tradition or sentiment in their favour (although the dislike for them seems to have recently diminished), and they have the initial disadvantages (which in 1871 seem to have been thought fatal to them) that more than a quarter of them cut the county boundaries, sometimes in a very complicated way; that they seldom coincide with boroughs or local board districts, or with highway districts; that the rectification of their areas would in many cases seriously disturb the burden of rates, and that some rectification may be necessary in many cases.

On the other hand, the unions start with this not inconsiderable presumption in their favour, that they have been formed within the last forty years, and formed deliberately for a purpose of local administration—and that a purpose which of all the then purposes of local administration the most demanded a strong and active administrative body, and a not unwieldy area—and formed systematically by one central authority acting presumably on one principle, so far as it seemed applicable after local inquiry in the interested localities. Something is no doubt detracted from the weight of this consideration by the admitted circumstances that there was in 1834 a more pressing need for getting the principle of the poor-law union accepted in some form than for getting the best areas accepted; that local influences, and the accidents of situation of workhouses, were necessarily permitted to make themselves felt; that in many cases the grouping, which was convenient thirty or forty years ago, has become inconvenient, or not the most convenient, through changes of population and of the means of communication, and that in many more cases the carving out of urban districts from rural unions has left the remains of the latter in a disjected condition. Whether these objections apply to so many cases and in so serious a degree as to disqualify the union for being the *basis* on which administrative areas should be constituted possibly cannot be determined without systematic inquiry. But, at any rate, no general complaint seems ever to have been made that the unions are either too large or too small, or that they have been otherwise inconveniently arranged. They have the advantages of an existing representative constitution which can easily be modified so far as may be necessary; they have capable officers acquainted with much of the various business of administration; and they are accustomed to central control and audit. Lastly, Parliament has, to a certain extent, committed itself to their adoption by adding to their original functions of poor relief the important functions of the rural sanitary authority, and, in the absence of school boards, large powers with reference to elementary education.

These considerations appear to warrant the acceptance of the union or rural sanitary district as the basis of rural local government, subject to such rectifications and modifications as may be found expedient to be made either by one comprehensive commission or by the gradual action of the Local Government Board. The principal modifications which might be necessary seem to be as follows:— *Alterations required if Union is adopted.*

    (i.) If the future County Board is to be constituted for the county as it now exists, and if the principle is adopted that the larger unit should be a simple aggregate of primary units, the unions extending into more counties than one must be divided, and the parts must be either made separate unions or merged in others. The legislation of 1876 and 1879 has given whatever powers were wanting for this purpose. Out of about 617 non-metropolitan unions, about 441 are wholly comprised each in one county. Out of the 176 unions which extend into several counties, the parts which extend into a different county from that in which the bulk of the population is situate have in 88 cases a population of less than 1,000, and in 47 other cases less than 5,000, and might probably be merged in other unions. In the 46 other cases (some of which are wholly urban) the population of the outlying part exceeds 5,000. In some of these cases, there will no doubt be some inconvenience in disturbing the existing unions. But even if it should be thought expedient in certain of these cases to preserve the existing unions, with special provisions for representation on the County Boards of the several counties into which they respectively extend, this does not appear to furnish a valid argument against simplification of areas and authorities in that great majority of cases in which no such special difficulties exist.

    (ii.) Boroughs and local board districts (except such small ones as may be dissolved or merged) should probably be constituted separate unions. But this change, which seems desirable for administrative simplicity, may involve a considerable disturbance of the burden of poor relief. The effect of the Union Chargeability Act was in many cases to spread the charge of the urban poor over an area including rural parishes, and the proposed change would in these cases again throw the whole burden of the urban poor on the urban parts of the union (*a*). It would, perhaps, be difficult to suggest a satisfactory settlement of this difficulty if the present system of indoor relief is to be continued. But the difficulty would practically disappear if for the purposes of indoor relief counties or groups of unions were substituted for the present unions. Such a substitution has much to recommend it on other grounds as a measure of economy and for the improvement of the administration of poor relief. If it were made, a contribution towards the necessary costs of indoor relief might be one of the best forms of public grants in aid of local expenditure, because it would give a direct and powerful stimulus to the general enforcement of the recognized principles on which poor relief ought to be given (*b*).

NOTES.

Union chargeability.

Note (*a*). There are many reasons for doubting whether the present system of union chargeability is just. Where a union is partly urban and partly rural an equal poor-rate for all the purposes of poor relief can hardly be fair, except by accident. A town, included in a larger union, may and often does contribute to the poor-rates in a much smaller proportion than that in which it supplies the paupers. To this it is to be added that the farmer in the rural parish pays poor-rates on a rateable value which equals or perhaps exceeds his probable net income, while the townsman pays on a rateable value which may bear a small proportion to income. Sufficient answers to these objections may be forthcoming in many cases ; but it seems probable that on the whole a fairer adjustment would be made by enlarging the area which is to bear what may be called the inevitable part of poor relief, which is substantially the indoor relief, and by leaving only the outdoor relief to fall on the smaller area.

Overlapping boroughs, &c.

Note (*b*). The cases of municipal Boroughs and Local board or Improvement Act districts which extend into more counties than one may seem at first sight to present an almost insuperable difficulty in the way of complete simplification as between the county and the primary unit. But on examination it will be seen that there are few such cases (35 in all), and that those in which any real difficulty can arise are fewer still. The following table of all the overlapping boroughs is abstracted from the Census of 1881 :—

MUNICIPAL BOROUGHS IN MORE COUNTIES THAN ONE.

Name.	Population in principal County.	Population in second County.
1. Abingdon	5,676	8
2. Burton-on-Trent	32,675	6,613
3. Bristol	143,548	63,326
4. Cardigan	2,727	942
5. Oxford	34,980	284
6. Peterborough	18,957	2,271
7. Staleybridge	16,384	6,401
8. Stamford	7,602	1,171
9. Stockport	45,003	14,550
10. Sudbury	5,855	729
11. Tamworth	2,589	2,302
12. Thetford	3,228	804
13. Warrington	33,506	3,973
14. Yarmouth	37,151	9,008

There are also (besides Oxford, which is a local board district as well as a borough) 21 Local Board or Improvement Act districts in two counties, viz.: Banbury, Barnet, Crowle, Filey, Hinckley, Malton, Mossley, Newmarket, Todmorden, Tunbridge Wells, and 11 others. One of these (Mossley) is in three counties. In nearly all these cases it will be found that the population in the second county is of no serious magnitude.

In the majority of these cases probably the simplest plan would be to make a slight alteration of the county boundary. Bristol presents no difficulty, being already a county of a city. In the remaining cases it will be matter for local inquiry whether an alteration of the county boundary, or of the municipal or sanitary boundary, or an assimilation of constitution to that of counties of cities, would cause the least inconvenience. Whatever course may be necessary to be adopted, no argument affecting the general question can be drawn from these few exceptions.

B. *Local Authorities.*

Primary authorities.

This is, perhaps, the most important part of the subject. However great the intrinsic advantages are of simple and convenient areas, these may be of even more consequence as favourable conditions for obtaining the best administrative bodies. But the mere simplification of areas and rates and the consolidation of powers may be expected to have of themselves a favourable effect upon the governing bodies. If in each district, whether urban or rural, one body, acting either as a whole, or by committees, is made the authority for the purposes of the sanitary laws, the roads, licensing, poor relief, and elementary education, the importance and interest of office in such a body will be greatly enhanced, and this will of itself go far to secure that the work will be well done, even if no other change is made. Beyond this, the principal change which has been at various times* suggested is, that the interest and voting-power of owners of property, as distinguished from occupiers, should be made less invidious in form and more certain in operation, and the duration of office extended. Owners already have the power of claiming a distinct voting-power in elections of the elective members of boards of guardians and in elections of local boards; but something more than the mere power of claiming a right to be registered appears to be necessary in order to induce the owners to exercise their power.

* Mr. Goschen's Committee of 1870 and Bill of 1871.

County Boards.

Assuming the constitution of districts and of primary authorities to be simplified, the necessary conditions will exist for the constitution of County Boards. The proposals which have come before Parliament for the establishment of such Boards have been based on two distinct grounds. One ground has been the demand of the ratepayers that the county business as it now exists shall be administered no longer by a body entirely nominated by the Crown, and substantially representing only one class of the community, but shall be administered by a body in which the tenants and ratepayers shall be directly represented. The other ground has been that it is desirable to create bodies intermediate between the primary Local Authorities and the Executive Government, with powers for dealing with matters in which the various Local Authorities within a county have common or conflicting interests, and desirable also to transfer to such a body, acting with local knowledge and representing the various local interests, some portion of the work of control or supervision exercised by the Local Government Board, and perhaps even some portion of the functions of Parliament in relation to local legislation. If the former of these two grounds stood alone, it might perhaps be sufficient to associate with the justices, when sitting in special or quarter sessions for administrative business, a certain number of elected guardians and representatives of Town Councils and Local Boards. But for the purposes of the second kind such an expedient may be insufficient, and it will therefore probably be necessary to constitute the County Board in a more substantially representative form. The settlement of its constitution will, however, mainly depend on the nature and amount of the work to be done by the reorganized county authority.

If a County Board is to exist more than in name, it seems clear that it must take over the entire administrative work of the Quarter Sessions. It must have the control and direction of valuation for the purposes not only of whatever rate will hereafter represent the existing county rate, but also, if rates are to be consolidated, of all rates and contributions; and it will be one of its most important and difficult functions to see that the existing inequalities and discrepancies in valuation in different unions are removed. It must also have the management of asylums and perhaps also of workhouses and of indoor relief. It must maintain the county buildings and deal with the county debt. It will probably, by itself or its committees, have to undertake the grant of licenses to sell intoxicating liquors. It will have the charge of county bridges and of so much of the administration of roads as may not be vested in the primary Local Authorities. It should also have power by schemes (to be valid if not disallowed by Parliament) to group, divide, and merge the existing districts and rectify boundaries and apportion property, debts, and officers—matters of great practical difficulty. It should also, perhaps, exercise powers of approving, and to some extent controlling, the annual estimates or budgets of the primary Local Authorities. It will have to watch and from time to time to intervene in inquiries and legislation affecting watersheds, drainage and rivers. And as experience shows that new work and duties continually come into existence for bodies capable of undertaking them, it may be expected that in the course of a few years many other important matters will come within its province, including probably some share in the work of Private Bill legislation. It, therefore, does not appear likely that there will be any want of business various and important enough to require all the strength which can be given to the constitution of the Board.

Business to be assigned to County Boards.

C. Local Rates.

Proposals for alterations in local taxation.

There are some alterations in local taxation on which the authorities are agreed, and which have been affirmed by committees or commissions and to some extent by Parliament itself. One of them is the consolidation of the rates leviable in each unit. Another is, that the system of valuation and assessment requires both simplification and some better means of ensuring uniformity in ascertaining the rack-rent value and in the deductions by which that value is brought down to "gross estimated rental," and from that to "net rateable value," and some provision for more cheap and periodical revision (*a*). A third, perhaps, is that the disbursement of all rates in each unit should be under one control and subject to one audit, and that accounts of the receipts, disbursements and liabilities should be prepared and published, so far as may be, on one uniform plan throughout the country, and for the same periods of account.

Consolidation of rates.

With regard, indeed, to the consolidation of rates, it is not easy to see how this is to be effected so long as the difference in the basis of assessment between the "general district-rate," with its exemption of agricultural land, railways, &c., to the extent of three-fourths, and the poor rate and other rates which admit no such exemption, is maintained. Nor is it easy, without better information as to the distribution of expenditure, to discover how far the extension or abolition of the three-fourths exemption would work injustice, or in what way any such injustice could best be made good. Perhaps the best temporary solution will be that there should be, at least for a time, two parts of the consolidated rate, one part with the exemption, and another without the exemption.

Rating of Owners.
* See Mr. Goschen's Committee of 1870 and Bill of 1871.

A proposal * about which there is less unanimity is, that at least some part of the local taxation should be charged immediately upon the owner instead of the occupier, and this on two main grounds,—the first, that under the existing law, where leases exist, any increase of

NOTE (*a*). Mr. Sclater-Booth, in introducing his Valuation Bill on 12th February, 1876, quoted Sir E. Kerrison as follows :—"* * * Even if a subsidy be given by Parliament in relief of local taxation, it cannot be fairly distributed while the rateable value of the same property in different unions varies from 10 to 40 per cent. * * *" See also his speech on introducing his Bill of 1877 (13th February, 1877).

taxation must, during the currency of the lease (however long it may be) fall exclusively upon the occupier—with especial hardship in times of exceptional depression; the second, that whilst it is desirable to interest owners as well as occupiers in local administration and economy, owners have no obvious and immediate motive for interfering in it so long as they do not directly feel the burden of increased taxation. These arguments appear to be *primâ facie* sufficient to establish the expediency of a prospective enactment of this kind. On the other hand, there are obvious objections against applying it indiscriminately to all kinds of rates or to all existing leases. Possibly a distinction may be supported between leases not originally exceeding twenty-one years and leases for a longer term; and it may be that even if the enactment is thought not to be properly applicable to existing leases for a short term, it might, without injustice, become applicable after a certain period of grace to longer leases, especially perhaps those which commenced before the great modern increase in taxation.

Another suggestion has been made for rendering more equitable the incidence of an important part of local burdens, both urban and rural. *New system of special charges.* The expenses of gas and water are already to a great extent, and in many cases, paid for, not by a rate strictly so called, but by a charge made on those only who consume them and in proportion to their consumption. It is proposed, so far as possible, to extend this principle, and in particular to apply it to sewerage by charging the cost of the sewers on the premises which do or might derive benefit from them, and resorting to a general rate only for so much of the private charge as would otherwise be excessive. It seems plain that this principle, so far as it can be applied, may be preferable to that of special districts, which must always be arbitrarily formed, and may be made a means of great injustice. The portion of the local expenditure to which the principle is or can be applied (subject to a difficulty mentioned below) seems to be, at present, about five millions a year; and as works of sewerage and water supply extend themselves over the rural districts and in new urban districts, the proportion of expenditure to which it is applicable may continually assume a greater importance as compared with the total local expenditure. It seems probable that the adoption of this principle will render it possible to carry out works of this kind in places in which they would be otherwise impracticable; and it will often furnish an answer to the most serious and well-founded objections to compulsory works of sewerage. The difficulty above referred to regards only existing works. So far as the annual charge for now existing water or sewerage works represents the cost of construction, as distinguished from that of maintenance and supply, the burden of the charge cannot be shifted from the ratepayer to the consumer without the consumer's consent. But this does not preclude the application of the principle to so much of the charge as represents maintenance and supply. It would only be necessary that in the demand-note the charge in respect of capital should be stated separately—a change which seems desirable in itself as regards the whole annual charge of the debt of any district.

Franchises, how far affected by alterations.

Provision will be necessary with regard to the parliamentary and municipal franchises. They must, to some extent, be interfered with by any considerable alteration in the mode of assessing and collecting rates, and this interference must be accepted as one of the necessary incidents of a reform in these respects. But the necessary interference will be reduced to very small dimensions if, as above suggested, the consolidated rate is levied in two parts. One of them would substantially represent the same thing as the existing poor and borough rates on which the parliamentary and municipal franchises are now based.

Conclusion.

In conclusion, it may be observed that as the local authorities are strengthened and the impediments to their good working removed, the necessity for interference by the central authority will be diminished, at the same time that the use and value of its supervision and of the information which it could communicate will be greatly increased. The existing confusion of things at once creates a necessity for perpetual interference, and makes the interference ineffectual.

APPENDIX.

Special Matters.

		PAGE
I.—BRIDGES	.	106
II.—PRISONS	.	106
III.—WEIGHTS AND MEASURES, &c.	.	107
IV.—CONTAGIOUS DISEASES (ANIMALS)	.	108
V.—REGISTRATION OF BIRTHS AND DEATHS	.	108
VI.—VACCINATION	.	109
VII.—PUBLIC BATHS AND WASHHOUSES	.	109
VIII.—PUBLIC LIBRARIES AND MUSEUMS	.	109
IX.—LIGHTING	.	110
X.—TRAMWAYS	.	111
XI.—ARTISANS AND LABOURERS' DWELLINGS	.	111
XII.—FACTORIES AND WORKSHOPS	.	113
XIII.—MISCELLANEOUS SANITARY POWERS	.	114
XIV.—FISHERY DISTRICTS	.	114
XV.—MARINE AND HARBOUR BOARDS	.	115
XVI.—TAX COMMISSIONERS	.	115

Note.

This Appendix deals with matters of minor importance locally administered. They are grouped as far as possible according to the districts in which they are administered. See the following table:—

TABLE.

SUBJECT-MATTER.	PRINCIPAL AREAS OF ADMINISTRATION.
I.—Bridges II.—Prisons III.—Weights and Measures IV.—Contagious Diseases	County and Borough.
V.—Registration VI.—Vaccination	Union.
VII.—Baths VIII.—Libraries IX.—Lighting X.—Tramways XI.—Artisans' Dwellings	Rural Parish and Urban Sanitary District.
XII.—Factories XIII.—Sanitary Powers	Urban and Rural Sanitary District.
XIV.—Fisheries XV.—Harbours XVI.—Taxes	Special Districts.

I.—BRIDGES.

1530, c. 5.
1702, c. 12.
1739, c. 29.
1741, c. 33.
1803, c. 59.
1812, c. 110.
1814, c. 90.
1815, c. 143.
1835, c. 50, s. 21.
1841, c. 49.
1870, c. 73.
1878, c. 77, ss. 21, 22.
1880, (2) c. 5.
1882, c. 50, s. 119.

AT common law the inhabitants of a county at large are *primâ facie* liable to repair all public bridges in the county. (2 Coke, Inst. 700.) But by usage, prescription or ancient tenure, hundreds, parishes, townships, corporations or individuals, may be liable to repair. (See *R.* v. *Hendon*, 4 B. & Ad. 628 ; *R.* v. *Ecclesfield*, 1 B. & Ald. 359.)

Under the Statute of Bridges (22 Hen. VIII., c. 5) and the amending Acts, the general liability to repair public bridges, if outside cities and towns corporate, is imposed on the inhabitants of the county, if inside, on the inhabitants of such city or town. In a county the justices in quarter sessions, and in a municipal borough the town council, superintend the repair, maintenance, alteration and improvement of such bridges, and may borrow money for these purposes. The expenses are charged and loans secured on the county and borough rate respectively. But no bridge built by a private person or corporation after 1803 is to be repairable by the county, unless built under the superintendence of the county surveyor, or accepted by the justices.

The approaches to any public bridge for the space of 300 feet on each side, are repairable by the same authority as the bridge, except in case of bridges built after the 20th March, 1836, when the approaches and road over the bridge are repairable by the highway, turnpike or other authority who were previously liable to repair the road.

1870, s. 12.

Where a turnpike road has become a highway, the bridges become county bridges, but the roads over them are repairable by the highway authority. (See Ch. VIII., p. 37).

II.—PRISONS.

1865, c. 126.
1877, c. 21.

UNDER the Prisons Act, 1865, the justices of a county, and the town council of a borough were, as the "prison authority," entrusted with the provision, control, and management of prisons. But the Prisons Act, 1877, provided that after the 1st April, 1878, the property in and superintendence of prisons should pass to the "Prison Commissioners" appointed by the Secretary of State, and the expenses of prisons should be paid out of the Parliamentary votes.

The effect of this change, as far as can be ascertained from the returns, has been to reduce the number of prisons by more than one-third (from 113 to 67), and the cost of prisoners by about £3 a head, or £58,000 a year. (See Parly. Paper, $\frac{1880}{370}$.)

The only powers now left to the old "prison authorities" are those relating to reformatory and industrial schools (see Ch. XII. p. 54).

1877, ss. 13—15.

But a visiting committee of justices is to be annually appointed by the justices of a county or liberty in quarter sessions, or the justices of a borough at special sessions, according to rules made by the Secretary of State. This Committee is to visit the local prisons, authorize certain punishments, and report to the Secretary of State.

III.—WEIGHTS AND MEASURES, &c.

Under the Weights and Measures Act, 1878, the local authority in every county and borough provide local standards of measure and weight, and means for verifying weights and measures by comparison with such standards. They also appoint inspectors of weights and measures, and allot them districts, make bye-laws (with the approval of the Board of Trade) for regulating their duties and fix the fees to be taken. 1878, c. 49.

The local authority in a county are Quarter Sessions and in a borough the town council, but in a borough not having a separate Court of Quarter Sessions the County Quarter Sessions are the local authority, unless the town council resolve to be such authority or have before 1878 provided standards and appointed inspectors.

The expenses are paid out of the county or borough rate and all fees taken go to that rate, but boroughs having their own inspectors do not contribute to the expenses of the county. 1882, c. 50, s. 152.

Besides the local authorities under the Act, other bodies (vestries, commissioners, borough justices, &c.) have under local Acts or charters authority in respect of weights and measures. 1878, ss. 54, 55, 63, 69.

Under the Sale of Gas Acts the local authority are to provide gas-meters, stamps, &c., and appoint inspectors for enforcing the Act. The local authority are the justices in quarter sessions for a county, and the town council for a borough, but the borough justices are substituted for a town council which itself supplies gas. *Gas Inspectors.* 1859, (2) c. 66. 1860, c. 146.

The Acts only treat as separate areas those boroughs which were in 1859 "county towns where gas is used," or in which the local authority have resolved to adopt the Act at some time previously to the 13th April 1861. When adopted the Acts supersede all like powers under local Acts. The expenses are paid out of "the county stock," and in boroughs out of the lighting or borough rate.

Under the Gasworks Clauses Act, 1871 (which applies to all future gas undertakings unless specially excluded), "the local authority of any district," not themselves supplying gas, may appoint gas examiners to test the gas supplied. 1871, c. 41, s. 29.

In certain counties (Yorkshire, Lancashire, Suffolk, &c.), a committee of woollen and yarn manufacturers may appoint inspectors to prevent frauds in those industries, and in the West Riding of Yorkshire, the justices in quarter sessions may appoint searchers and measurers of cloth for like purposes. *Yarn Inspectors.* 1777, c. 11. 1784, c. 3. 1785, c. 40. 1791, c. 56. 1765, c. 51. 1766, c. 23.

Under the Sale of Food and Drugs Acts, analysts may be appointed for boroughs having a separate Court of Quarter Sessions or a separate police *Analysts.* 1875, c. 63. 1879, c. 30.

IV.—CONTAGIOUS DISEASES (ANIMALS).

1878, c. 74.

For the purposes of the Contagious Diseases (Animals) Act, 1878, the local authorities and rates are in boroughs (generally speaking) the council and the borough rate, and elsewhere the quarter sessions and county rate. The local authority may act by a committee and sub-committees. They appoint and pay inspectors and other officers. They may provide places for the reception and slaughter of imported animals. They have large powers for the inspection and slaughter (with compensation) of diseased animals and animals likely to be infected, and for prohibiting removal of animals and for compelling disinfection. The Privy Council exercise a general control by orders.

Boroughs assessed to a county rate are to be exempted from any county rate levied under this Act. If a rate under this Act would exceed 6d. in the £, the whole may be borrowed for a period of seven years. If it would exceed 9d., the period may be extended to fourteen years. The loan may be obtained from the Public Works Loan Commissioners.

1877, c. 68.

The above-mentioned authorities and rates, are also the authorities and rates for the Destructive Insects Act, 1877.

V.—REGISTRATION OF BIRTHS AND DEATHS.

1836, c. 86.
1837, c. 22.
1858, c. 25.
1865, c. 79, s. 1.
1874, c. 88.

The district for Registration purposes is *primâ facie* the poor-law "union." The guardians are required to divide their district into sub-districts and appoint a registrar in each sub-district, and a superintendent registrar for the whole district. The Registrar General, however, with the approval of the Local Government Board, may unite, divide, or alter districts for registration purposes, and declare what board of guardians shall appoint the superintendent registrar for a united district. The registrars and superintendents are removable by the Registrar General, who exercises a general control. The fees of registrars and expenses of registry offices are paid by the board of guardians out of the common fund for poor-law purposes, and in united districts the several boards contribute in proportion to the population of their respective areas.

1880 (2), c. 37.

These Registration Districts and sub-districts formed are also the units for taking the decennial census. In 1881, they were 601 in number (besides 29 in the metropolis), and coincided with the Poor Law Unions or incorporations formed under local Acts, except in about 30 cases where unions were combined for registration purposes. (See Census 1881, vol. II.)

VI.—VACCINATION.

The guardians in each poor-law "union" are (generally speaking) the local authority for the enforcement of the Vaccination Acts, subject to the control of the Local Government Board. Each union is ordinarily divided into vaccination districts, for each of which at least one public vaccinator is appointed, towards whose remuneration an allowance is made by the Treasury. There are also vaccination officers who are charged with all duties of registering vaccinations, &c. These officers are appointed by the guardians, subject to the control of the Local Government Board. Vaccination expenses are payable out of the common (poor) fund of the union.

1867, c. 84.
1871, c. 98.
1874, c. 75.

VII.—PUBLIC BATHS AND WASHHOUSES.

The Baths and Washhouses Acts are adoptive only. They may be adopted in any urban sanitary district, and, with the approval of a Secretary of State, in any "parish." Their purpose is explained by their title. The local authority for their execution is, in an urban district, the sanitary authority, and the expenses fall (speaking generally) on the general district rate. In rural parishes which adopt the Acts the local authority is a body of commissioners appointed by the vestry, and the expenses fall on the poor rate, but cannot exceed such amount as the vestry sanction from time to time. In these Acts "parish" means a poor-law parish with separate overseers and also "any place maintaining its own poor and having a vestry."

1846, c. 74.
1847, c. 61.
1875, c. 55, s. 10.
1878, c. 14.
1882, c. 30.

VIII.—PUBLIC LIBRARIES AND MUSEUMS.

The Public Libraries Act, 1855, and amending Acts, may be adopted by a two-thirds majority of a public meeting in any urban sanitary district, or parish, or group of parishes having (in any of the above cases) 5,000 population. When adopted it is to be executed in a borough by the council, at the cost of the borough rate or of a special borough rate; or in an improvement act district, by its improvement commissioners, at the cost either of the improvement rate or of a special rate; or in a local board district, by the local board, at the cost of the general district rate; or in a parish, by elected commissioners, at the cost of a special poor rate, with an exemption of agricultural land, &c. to the extent of *two-thirds*. Any rate or expenditure under this Act is limited to one penny in the £. The adoption of the Acts may be by voting papers, which may stipulate for a lower rate than that limited by the Acts.

The purposes of the Acts include libraries, museums and schools of science or art. The local authority may act through committees, the members of which need not be members of that authority.

1855, c. 70.
1866, c. 114.
1871, c. 71.
1877, c. 54.

IX.—LIGHTING.

<small>1833, c. 90.
1851, c. 50.</small>

The Lighting and Watching Act, 1833, may be adopted in any parish or part of a parish (rural or urban), and either as to lighting or watching or both by a majority of two-thirds of the ratepayers. It provides for the election by the qualified ratepayers of Inspectors, one-third of whom go out of office annually. The inspectors may appoint officers and watchmen, erect watchhouses, and provide fire-engines, lamps, gas, &c. The inspectors of adjoining parishes may unite for the better execution of the Act. The expenses are paid out of a rate levied like the poor-rate on the precept of the inspectors, but houses, buildings, and property other than land are to be rated at three times as much as land. The maximum amount of expenditure is previously fixed by a vote of the ratepayers. An appeal lies to quarter sessions from any order of the inspectors and any rate made under the Act.

<small>1835, c. 76,
s. 84 (repealed).
1840, c. 88.</small>

This Act, so far as it relates to watching, has now been superseded both in counties and boroughs by the Police Acts (see Ch. IX. p. 44), though outside boroughs inspectors under the old Act may still levy rates for additional constables supplied under s. 20 of the County Police Act, 1840.

<small>1875, c. 55,
s. 163.</small>

For lighting purposes, this Act in 1882, still applied to 192 places, mostly small and semi-rural, but including the large borough of Leeds. The Lighting and Watching rates in these places for the year 1881-82 amounted to £36,266. It is expressly provided by the Public Health Act that the Lighting and Watching Act shall be superseded in any place which after the passing of that Act becomes included in an urban sanitary district. It may also be superseded at any time in any sanitary district by an order of the Local Government Board.

<small>*Gas Supply.*
1875, c. 55.
ss. 161—163.</small>

In an urban sanitary district the sanitary authority may under the Public Health Act, 1875, either contract for the supply of gas, &c., and provide lamps and other materials, or themselves supply gas in a district not already supplied, or purchase the undertaking of a gas company. In the two last cases they must obtain the sanction of the Local Government Board.

<small>*Electric
Lighting.*
1882, c. 56.</small>

Under the Electric Lighting Act, 1882, any urban or rural sanitary authority may apply to the Board of Trade for a licence or provisional order to supply electricity in any part of their district, and may when so authorized sub-contract with any company, &c. for such supply. The same authorities have also considerable control over other electric undertakings within their district, and a right to purchase them on special terms after 21 years. The expenses are in the case of an urban authority to be charged on (speaking generally) the general district rate, in the case of a rural authority to be levied as "special expenses" on the contributory places benefited (see Ch. VII., p. 30).

X.—TRAMWAYS.

The "local authority," under the Tramways Act, 1870, may apply for a provisional order, and construct tramways, and lease them when constructed, or take tolls for their use. They may also regulate by bye-law, and in certain cases purchase the tramways of other undertakers. The "local authority" is the sanitary authority in an urban sanitary district, and elsewhere the vestry or other body of persons acting as a vestry. The expenses are paid out of the sanitary-rate and poor-rate respectively. 1870, c. 78.

Certain powers of removing tramways when disused are noted in the "road authority," *i.e.*, the highway board or other body maintaining the roads. No new tramway can be made without the consent of both the "local authority" and the "road authority."

XI.—ARTISANS AND LABOURERS' DWELLINGS.

Public or private powers for the provision, improvement, or regulation of Labourers' Dwellings are given under five classes of Acts, namely :—

Public bodies
- A. The "Labouring Classes Lodging-Houses" Acts.
- B. The "Artisans and Labourers' Dwellings" Acts.
- C. The Public Health Act, 1875.

Private bodies or persons
- D. The Improvement of Land Act, 1864.
- E. The "Labourers' Dwellings" Acts.

It seems desirable to notice the two latter classes, although their provisions have not, strictly speaking, any relation to local government.

A. *The "Labouring Classes Lodging-Houses" Acts.*

The purpose of these Acts is to encourage the provision of improved lodging houses for the labouring classes. 1851, c. 34.
1866, c. 28.
1867, c. 28.

The Act of 1851 may be adopted in any urban sanitary district, and in such districts the sanitary authority is the local authority for the execution of the Act. It may also, with the approval of a Secretary of State, be adopted by any parish with 10,000 population, or separately by any parish in a borough with the like population, or by several parishes uniting for this purpose, and having the like aggregate population; and in these cases the local authority is to be a body of commissioners appointed by the vestry or vestries, or the urban sanitary authority. The local authority has power to buy land by agreement and to build lodging-houses, or to buy existing lodging-houses. The Act of 1866, which authorizes public loans to the local authorities under the Act of 1851, seems to extend their powers to the provision of labourers' dwellings of any kind. 1875, c. 55, s. 10.

The expenses are borne in urban districts out of the sanitary rate (speaking generally), and in other places out of the poor-rate.

1882, c. 50. s. 111.
Further, by the Municipal Corporations Act, 1882, municipal corporations are empowered, with the sanction of the Treasury, to grant leases for 999 years of corporate land for sites for working men's dwellings.

B. *The "Artisans and Labourers' Dwellings" Acts.*

There are two groups of these Acts, both applying only to urban districts, the first relating to small local improvements, the second providing for the clearance and rebuilding of wider areas.

1868, c. 130.
1879, c. 64.
1882. c. 54,
ss. 7—11.
"The Artisans Dwellings Acts, 1868 to 1882," (Torrens' Acts), apply to all urban districts. The local authority is the urban sanitary authority. The purpose of these Acts is to provide for the alteration or demolition of houses so dangerous to health as to be unfit for habitation, and of adjoining houses obstructing ventilation or otherwise contributing to the evil. The local authority may be compelled to purchase any house included in their order, or the owner may execute the alterations himself, or the local authority may execute them in his default. Where the local authority purchase, they may alter, improve, and regulate by bye-laws the houses so belonging to them. An appeal lies from any Order of the local authority to the Court of Quarter Sessions. The expenses of executing these Acts (so far as they are not recoverable from the owners, or chargeable on the premises improved) are (speaking generally) paid out of the general district rate, but the increase of that rate for this purpose is limited to 2*d.* in the £.

1875, c. 36.
1879, c. 63.
1882, c. 54,
ss. 1—6.
"The Artisans and Labourers' Dwellings Improvement Acts, 1875 to 1882," (Sir R. Cross's Acts) apply only to urban districts with a population of 25,000. The local authority is the urban sanitary authority. The purpose of these Acts is to provide for the compulsory purchase and clearance by the local authority of unhealthy areas in towns, and for the execution of improvement schemes (when sanctioned by Provisional Order) in such areas. The cost, in so far as it is not met by the proceeds of the sale or lease of the land for the purposes of the scheme, is to be borne (speaking generally) by the general district rate.

C. *The Public Health Act,* 1875.

1875. c. 55.
ss. 157—160.
ss. 71—90.

s. 314.
1882, c. 23.
1883, c. 41, s. 9.
This Act, besides empowering urban sanitary authorities to regulate new buildings, improve streets, remove dangerous buildings, &c., also enables any sanitary authority (whether urban or rural) to close cellar dwellings, register and regulate by bye-laws common lodging-houses, and also by the order of the Local Government Board ordinary lodging-houses. Any sanitary authority may also make bye-laws for the decent lodging of persons engaged in picking hops, fruit or vegetables within their district.

Under the Merchant Shipping Act, 1883, the sanitary authority of any seaport town may, with the sanction of the Board of Trade, make bye-laws for licensing and regulating seamen's lodgings.

D. *Improvement of Land Act*, 1864.

The purposes of this Act include "the erection of labourers' cottages," and "the improvement of and addition to labourers' cottages," but with a view only to the permanent improvement *of the value* of private estates. For these purposes life-owners and other owners of land for long but limited terms are enabled, with the sanction and under the control of the Inclosure Commissioners to charge the inheritance or reversion of the land. The Public Works Loan Commissioners could not under the Act of 1869 advance money for these purposes, and it may be doubted whether the Public Works Loans Act, 1875, applies for this purpose. But now by the Settled Land Act, 1882, limited owners may sell settled lands and invest the proceeds in certain authorized classes of improvements, including labourers' cottages.

_{1864, c. 114.}

_{1882, c. 38.}

E. *The "Labourers' Dwellings" Acts.*

The purposes of the Act of 1855 is to facilitate the establishment of private companies, with limited liability, for providing dwellings for the labouring classes, with power to hold land not exceeding ten acres, and to buy land by agreement under the Lands Clauses Act. The Local Government Board have powers for regulating and inspecting such dwellings.

_{1855, c. 132.
1866, c. 28.
1879, c. 77, s. 6.}

By the Acts of 1866 and 1879, the Public Works Loan Commissioners are authorized to lend money on mortgage for the purposes of such dwellings to any company constituted for this purpose, or to any railway or trading company, or to owners of land in fee or for fifty years unexpired. These Acts do not give any such power of charging the inheritance or reversion as is given by the Improvement of Land Act.

XII.—FACTORIES AND WORKSHOPS.

The Factory and Workshop Acts were passed for the purpose of regulating the safety, sanitary conditions, &c., of factories and workshops in both urban and rural places. They are in general executed by inspectors appointed by a Secretary of State. But the (urban or rural) sanitary authority is bound to enforce the law on receiving a notice from an inspector of a nuisance existing in any factory or workshop; and the execution of the provisions relating to the sanitary conditions of retail bakehouses is entrusted exclusively to the sanitary authority.

_{1878, c. 16, ss. 3, 4, 33—35.
1883, c. 53, s. 15—18.}

Under the Public Health Act, 1875, any factory, workshop, or workplace, if not properly cleansed and ventilated, or over-crowded, becomes a nuisance abateable summarily on complaint of the sanitary authority. A furnace of a factory, &c., not consuming (as far as is practicable) its own smoke, is a nuisance abatable in like manner.

_{1875, c. 55, ss. 91—96.}

Under an Act of 1872, the same authority may sanction the use of steam-whistles in factories, subject to an appeal to the Local Government Board.

_{1872, c. 61.}

XIII.—MISCELLANEOUS SANITARY POWERS.

IN addition to those already mentioned, the following sanitary powers are exercised by the authorities constituted under the Public Health Act (see Ch. VII).

Canal Boats.
1877, c. 60.

(i.) Under the Canal Boats Act, 1877, the sanitary authority of any district abutting on a canal or river has power in certain cases to register and inspect canal boats.

Commons.
1876, c. 56, s. 8.

(ii.) By the Commons Act, 1876, the authority of an urban sanitary district containing not less than 5,000 inhabitants may acquire, contribute to the maintenance, or be invested with the management of any common in or within 6 miles of their district. The expenses are to be paid out of the sanitary rate.

Rivers Pollution.
1876, c. 75.

(iii.) The Rivers Pollution Prevention Act, 1876, provides penalties for polluting rivers, and requires sanitary authorities to afford facilities for drainage from manufactories into their sewers. Sanitary authorities may enforce the Act. Tidal waters are within this Act so far as the Local Government Board may determine.

Water-supply.
1878, c. 25.
See 1875, c. 55, s. 51.

(iii.) Under the Public Health (Water) Act, 1878, rural sanitary authorities have power to compel owners of houses to supply them properly with water. There is an appeal to the Local Government Board, who may charge the rural authority with part of the cost.

XIV.—FISHERY DISTRICTS.

1861, c. 109.
1865, c. 121.
1873, c. 71.
1876, c. 19.
1878, c. 39.
1884, c. .

UNDER the Salmon Fishery Acts, 1861 to 1876, and the Freshwater Fisheries Acts, 1878 and 1884, the Secretary of State on the application of the justices in Quarter Sessions, may order that any rivers in a county, which are frequented by salmon or any freshwater fish, shall form a fishery district, either separately or jointly with rivers of another county. Each fishery district has a board of conservators, consisting partly of *ex officio* members, partly of members annually appointed by the justices of the county in Quarter Sessions (or by a joint fishery committee of two or more counties), and partly of members annually elected by persons licensed to fish. This board issue licenses, make bye-laws as to close time, &c., appoint water-bailiffs, and generally enforce the laws for the protection of fish.

XV.—MARINE AND HARBOUR BOARDS.

A. LOCAL Marine Boards are established under the Merchant Shipping Act, 1854, in any seaports appointed by the Board of Trade. They consist of the mayor and stipendiary magistrate (if any), 4 members appointed by the Board of Trade, and 6 members elected by the qualified shipowners of the port. They make returns to the Board of Trade, and establish shipping offices for the registry and engagement of seamen, examination of masters, and other matters connected with the sea service. The expenses are paid out of the Mercantile Marine Fund, a fund raised by fees, dues, and harbour rates payable under the Merchant Shipping and Harbour Acts.

1854, c. 104. ss. 110—131.

s. 242.

B. There are also many Harbour Authorities, constituted either by special Acts incorporating all or some of the provisions of the Harbour Clauses Act, 1847, or by the Board of Trade's provisional orders under the General Pier and Harbour Acts. In 1882 there were 66 of these authorities, in England and Wales, with a revenue (excluding London) of 2¼ millions, chiefly raised by tonnage dues and tolls. Their outstanding debts amounted to 24½ millions. The Public Works Loan Commissioners are empowered to lend to Harbour authorities at a low rate of interest (see Ch. XVI., p. 70). For port sanitary authorities, see Ch. VII. p. 30.

1847, c. 27.
1861, c. 45.
1862, c. 19.

XVI.—TAX COMMISSIONERS.

THE districts formed for the collection of the imperial taxes have, as a rule, no connection with Local Government. But it seems desirable to notice shortly the local bodies that exist for the assessment of the land-tax, income-tax, and similar duties.

The Land Tax was originally (like other taxes) an aid periodically granted by Parliament, but by the Act of 1798 (c. 60), was converted into a perpetual charge on the land, subject to a right of redemption. This Act permanently fixed the "quotas" or amounts to be paid by each county, or division of a county, and by each town, parish, or place. It however provided (by s. 74, now replaced by s. 180 of the Act of 1802) for a new assessment of the unredeemed portion of the quota being annually made on the unredeemed lands within each "parish or place." (See *R.* v. *Tower Land Tax Commissioners,* 22 L. J. Q. B. 386).

Land-tax.
1798, c. 5,
c. 60, s. 1.
1802, c. 116
ss. 3, 180.
1827, c. 75.

The Land-tax Commissioners are appointed and named for "divisions," *i.e.*, counties and divisions of counties and certain large towns, by the Act of 1798 (c. 5), and various subsequent statutes. By the Act of 1827, all justices of the peace may act as such Commissioners. In all cases a certain property qualification (*e.g.*, £100 a year in land in counties) is required.

These Commissioners appoint assessors for each "parish or place" within their division, and hear appeals against assessments.

Income-tax.
1842, c. 35. s. 4.

The Land-tax Commissioners for each division, are directed by the Income-tax Act, 1842, and amending Acts (revived annually by the Customs and Inland Revenue Act) to appoint "General Commissioners" for the assessment of the income-tax, and inhabited house duties. These Commissioners are appointed and act for the several Inland Revenue districts. They must have similar (but somewhat higher) property qualifications to those of the Land-tax Commissioners. In certain special cases they are to appoint "additional Commissioners." None of the above Commissioners receive any remuneration, but if they do not perform their duties, the Treasury may appoint paid "special Commissioners," without any property qualification, to perform them.

1880, (2) c. 19, ss. 42-57.

Under the Taxes Management Act, 1880, the General Commissioners annually in April appoint certain inhabitants of each "parish or place" to be assessors, and order them to make their returns to the Commissioners in July. In default of other assessors the Inland Revenue surveyors act, and in any case these officers have to revise the assessments. The Commissioners allow the revised assessments, and hear appeals against them.

ss. 36, 37.

The Land-tax Commissioners of any division may unite or disunite "parishes" for tax purposes, and the same Commissioners at a general meeting for a county may transfer any "parish" (together with the quota of land tax chargeable on the parish at the time of transfer) from one division of the county to another, or constitute new divisions. The approval of the Treasury is necessary in either case.

INDEX OF PARLIAMENTARY PAPERS AND DEBATES.

A.—The most important Reports and Returns bearing on the subject of local government are the following :—

1. Commissioners' Report on Poor Laws, 1834.
2. Municipal Corporations Commission, first Report, 1835.
3. Report of Poor Law Commissioners on Local Taxation, 1843.
4. Duke of Buccleugh's Commission, 1844 (Large Towns and Populous Districts).
5. S. C. of H. of C. on County Finance, 1868.
6. Sanitary Commissions. Reports, 1868—72 (Sir C. Adderley).
7. S. C. of H. of C. on Local Taxation, 1870 (Mr. Goschen).
8. Mr. Goschen's Report on Local Taxation, 1870.
9. S. C. of H of C. on Parish and Union Boundaries, 1873 (Mr. Stansfeld).
10. S. C. of H. of L. on Highways, 1881 (Duke of Somerset).
11. Annual Reports of Local Government Board.
12. Annual Abstracts of Local Taxation Returns.
13. County Treasurers' Accounts.
14. Municipal Borough Accounts.

B.—The following are the dates of some of the most important debates on local government since 1869 :—

1870. Feb. 18 ; April 25.		Mr. Goschen's Bill. Poor Relief : Metropolis.
,, 21.		Mr. Goschen. Motion for S. C. on Local Taxation.
1871. ,, 28.		Sir M. Lopes. Motion : Local Burdens.
April. 3.		Mr. Goschen. Rating, &c. Bills.
May 5.		Mr. W. H. Smith. Poor Law : Metropolis.
1872. Feb. 16 ; April 5.		Mr. Stansfeld's Public Health Bill.
April 16.		Sir M. Lopes. Motion : Local Burdens.
1873. May 12.		Mr. Stansfeld. Motion for S. C. on Boundaries, &c.
1876. Feb. 12.		Mr. Sclater-Booth's Valuation Bill.
July 5.		Mr. Sclater-Booth's Public Works Loans Bill.
1877. Mar. 9.		Mr. Clare Read's Resolution for County Boards.
1878. Jan. 28. ⎫ Feb. 18. ⎬ Mar. 7. ⎭		Mr. Sclater-Booth's County Government Bill.
April 4, 12.	,, ,,	Public Works Loans Bill.
June 14, 17.	,, ,,	Valuation of Property Bill.
1879. Mar. 18.	,, ,,	County Boards Bill.
Aug. 9.	,, ,,	Public Works Loans Bill.
1880. Feb. 28.	,, ,,	Valuation of Property Bill.
1881. Mar. 28.		Mr. Harcourt. Motion : Maintenance of Main Roads.
May. 23.		Mr Pell. Motion for annual Statement of Local Taxation and Expenditure.
1882. Feb. 21.		Mr. Paget. Motion on Local Taxation.
1883. April 17.		Mr. Pell. Motion on Local Taxation.
1884. Mar. 28.		,, ,, ,,

INDEX OF SESSIONS.

(See note at p. xvi.)

N.B.—*These References are to the Revised Edition of the Statutes. The figure (2) denotes a second session in the same year.*

1275.—3 Edw. I.	1782.—22 Geo. III.	1848.—11 & 12 Vict.
1276.—4 Edw. I.	1784.—24 Geo. III. Sess. 2	1849.—12 & 13 Vict.
1285.—13 Edw. I.	1785.—25 Geo. III.	1850.—13 & 14 Vict.
	1786.—26 Geo. III.	1851.—14 & 15 Vict.
1340.—14 Edw. III.	1791.—31 Geo. III.	1852.—15 & 16 Vict.
1354.—28 Edw. III.	1796.—36 Geo. III.	1853.—16 & 17 Vict.
	1798.—38 Geo. III.	1854.—17 & 18 Vict.
1487.—3 Hen. VII.	1802.—42 Geo. III.	1855.—18 & 19 Vict.
	1808.—48 Geo. III.	1856.—19 & 20 Vict.
1530.—22 Hen. VIII.	1812.—52 Geo. III.	1857.—20 Vict.
1531.—23 Hen. VIII.	1816.—56 Geo. III.	1857 (2).—20 & 21 Vict.
1533.—25 Hen. VIII.	1818.—58 Geo. III.	1858.—21 & 22 Vict.
1545.—37 Hen. VIII.	1819.—59 Geo. III.	1859.—22 Vict.
		1859 (2).—22 & 23 Vict.
1549.—3 & 4 Edw. VI.	1820.—1 Geo. IV.	1860.—23 & 24 Vict.
	1825.—6 Geo. IV.	1861.—24 & 25 Vict.
1553.—1 Mary.	1826.—7 Geo. IV.	1862.—25 & 26 Vict.
	1827.—7 & 8 Geo. IV.	1863.—26 & 27 Vict.
1571.—13 Eliz.	1828.—9 Geo. IV.	1864.—27 & 28 Vict.
1601.—43 Eliz.	1829.—10 Geo. IV.	1865.—28 & 29 Vict.
		1866.—29 & 30 Vict.
1662.—14 Cha. II.	1831.—1 & 2 Will. IV.	1867.—30 & 31 Vict.
	1832.—2 & 3 Will. IV.	1868.—31 & 32 Vict.
	1833.—3 & 4 Will. IV.	1869.—32 & 33 Vict.
1688.—1 Will. & Mary.	1834.—4 & 5 Will. IV.	1870.—33 & 34 Vict.
	1835.—5 & 6 Will. IV.	1871.—34 & 35 Vict.
1702.—1 Anne.	1836.—6 & 7 Will. IV.	1872.—35 & 36 Vict.
1708.—7 Anne.		1873.—36 & 37 Vict.
	1837.—7 Will. IV. & 1 Vict.	1874.—37 & 38 Vict.
1723.—9 Geo. I.		1875.—38 & 39 Vict.
	1838.—1 & 2 Vict.	1876.—39 & 40 Vict.
1739.—12 Geo. II.	1839.—2 & 3 Vict.	1877.—40 & 41 Vict.
1741.—14 Geo. II.	1840.—3 & 4 Vict.	1878.—41 & 42 Vict.
1744.—17 Geo. II.	1841.—4 & 5 Vict.	1879.—42 & 43 Vict.
1750.—23 Geo. II.	1842.—5 & 6 Vict.	1880.—43 Vict.
1752.—25 Geo. II.	1843.—6 & 7 Vict.	1880 (2).—43 & 44 Vict.
	1844.—7 & 8 Vict.	1881.—44 & 45 Vict.
1765.—5 Geo. III.	1845.—8 & 9 Vict.	1882.—45 & 46 Vict.
1766.—6 Geo. III.	1846.—9 & 10 Vict.	1883.—46 & 47 Vict.
1777.—17 Geo. III.	1847.—10 & 11 Vict.	1884.—47 & 48 Vict.

GENERAL INDEX.

ADULTERATION. See *Analysts*.

ALDERMAN,
    of a borough, how chosen, 18

ANALYSTS,
    appointment of county and borough, 107

AREAS,
    of local government, complexity of, 93
        inconvenience of, 94
    what are the best primary, 95
    for special matters, 105

ARTISANS' DWELLINGS,
    provisions of, 111, 112

ASSESSMENT. See *Valuation*.
    made by overseers, 26
    for sewers rate, 62

ASSESSMENT COMMITTEE
    appointed by guardians, 9, 65

AUDIT
    of poor-law accounts, 10, 66
    of borough, etc., accounts, 67

BAKEHOUSES,
    regulation of, by sanitary authority, 113

BATHS,
    public, Acts relating to, 109

BILLIARDS,
    licenses for, 48

BOARD OF TRADE,
    powers of, 112, 115

BOROUGH RATE,
    how levied, 18

BOROUGHS,
    municipal, 17
    with separate commission, 18
    with separate quarter sessions, 18, 107
    contributions to county rate of, 19
    unreformed, 19
    number and boundaries of, 19, 59
    lunatic asylums in, 50, 52
    election of school boards in, 53
    burial boards in, 57
    appointment of auditors in, 66
    list of, with large debts, 86
    sanitary expenditure in, 88
    appointment of inspectors, &c. in, 107, 108

BRIDGES,
    when repairable by county or borough, 106

BURIAL BOARD,
    election and powers of, 56, 59

CABS,
    licensing of, 49

CANALS,
    police on, 45
    regulation of boats on, 114

CEMETERIES,
    provision of, 56
    consecration of, 59

CENSUS,
    districts for taking, 108

CHURCH BUILDING ACTS,
    provisions of, 6, 56

CHURCH RATE,
    where still compulsory, 7

CHURCHYARD,
    enlargement of, 56
    burials in, 60

CLERK OF THE PEACE,
    in a county, 13, 15
    in quarter sessions borough, 18

CLOTH,
    appointment of searchers of, 107

COLLECTOR
    of rates, 3

COMMONS,
    management of, by sanitary authority, 114

COMPOUNDING
    of rates, what is, 27

CONSTABLES,
    chief in a county, 42
    high, and parish, 42, 45
    special, 45
    additional, 45, 110

CONTAGIOUS DISEASES,
    of animals, 108

CORONER,
    county, 13, 15
    of quarter sessions borough, 18

CORPORATIONS,
    municipal, 17
    unreformed, 19

COUNCIL. See *Town Council*.

COUNTIES,
    number of, 12
    divisions of, 12, 15
    exceptionally organized, 15
    detached parts of, 14
    of towns, 20
    alteration of boundaries of, 99

COUNTY AUTHORITY,
    under Highways Act. 1878, 38
    expenditure by, 89

COUNTY BOARDS,
    reasons for creation of, 100
    business to be assigned to, 101

COUNTY PROPERTY,
    how vested, 15

COUNTY RATE.
    how made and raised, 14
    expenditure charged on, 14, 18, 106–108
    boroughs exempt from, 19, 20
    contribution out of, to main roads, 38
    bridges maintainable out of, 106

CUSTOS ROTULORUM,
    how appointed, 13

DISTRICT AUDITORS,
    appointment and payment of, 66

DOGS,
    control of, 49

DRAINAGE
> of land, 61—63

DRUNKARDS,
> licensing retreats for, 49

EDUCATION DEPARTMENT,
> control of schools by, 53

ELECTRICITY,
> supply of, by local authority, 110

EXPENDITURE,
> amount of local, 75, 80
> analysis of local, 89

EXPLOSIVES,
> licensing for, 49

FACTORIES,
> inspection and regulation of, 113

FISHERY DISTRICTS,
> formation of, 114

FRANCHISE,
> how far affected by alteration in rating, 104

GAME,
> licenses to sell, 48

GAS,
> expenditure on, in urban districts, 88, 90
> measuring and testing of, 107
> supply of, by local authority, 110

GENERAL DISTRICT RATE,
> how different from poor rate, 22, 30, 102
> where leviable, 32

GOVERNMENT CONTRIBUTIONS,
> amount of, 78, 80
> analysis of, 92
> in lieu of rates, 28, 92

GUARDIANS,
> duties of, 3, 4, 9, 10, 24, 106, 107
> election of, 9, 11
> expenses of, 27
> enforcement of the Education Acts by, 53
> provision of cemeteries by, 58
> alterations required in election of, 100

HARBOURS,
> authorities in, 115
> See *Port Sanitary Authorities.*

HIGHWAY
> authorities, 34—36
>> under Act of 1878, 38
> district, 35
> rate, 35, 36
>> valuation for, 39

HIGHWAYS,
> classes of, 34
> expenditure on, 39
> in South Wales, 41
> bridges on, how repairable, 104

HUNDREDS,
> division of counties into, 15
> repair of bridges and roads by, 39, 106
> constables for, 42

IMPROVEMENT ACT DISTRICTS,
> how constituted, 22

IMPROVEMENT ACTS,
> usual provisions of, 23

INCOME TAX,
> assessment of, 115, 116

INTOXICATING LIQUORS,
> licensing for, 47

JUSTICES,
> county, 12, 13, 15
>> jurisdiction over boroughs of, 18, 19
> borough, 18
> licensing powers of, 47
> administrative duties of, 49, 106—108

LABOURERS' DWELLINGS,
> provision of, 111—113

LAND,
> exemption of agricultural, etc., from rates, 22, 30, 109, 110
> improvement of, 113

LAND TAX,
> assessment of, 115

LIBERTIES,
> when treated as counties, 12, 15, 46, 47, 108

LIBRARIES,
> public, Acts relating to, 109

LICENSES
> for intoxicating liquors, billiards, etc., 47
> excise, 49

LIEUTENANT
> of a county, 13

LIGHTING
    by local authorities, 110

LOCAL ACCOUNTS,
    audit of, 66
    returns of, 67

LOCAL AUTHORITIES,
    analysis of expenditure of, 89—91

LOCAL BOARDS,
    election and duties of, 22, 23

LOCAL GOVERNMENT BOARD,
    poor-law powers of, 9, 10, 24, 25, 54
    sanitary powers of, 30, 32
    powers as to drainage of, 63
    appointment of auditors by, 66
    sanction of, required for loans, 70, 71

LOCAL GOVERNMENT DISTRICTS,
    number and boundaries of, 21, 23

LOCAL LOANS,
    how raised, 69
    rate of interest on, 71
    recent increase in amount of, 75, 76, 84—87
    possible amount of, 77

LOCAL MARINE BOARDS,
    constitution of, 115

LOCAL TAXATION,
    tables of, 75, 79
    amount of, compared with imperial taxes, 78
    proposed alterations in, 102

LOCAL TAXATION RETURNS,
    when made, 67, 73
    difficulties in, 73, 74

LOCOMOTIVES,
    regulation of, by county authority, 38, 39

LODGING HOUSES,
    provision and regulation of, 111, 112

LUNATIC ASYLUMS,
    licensing of, 50, 51

MAGISTRATES. See *Justices, Police Magistrate.*

MAIN ROADS
    under Highways Act, 1878, 37, 39

MAYOR
    of a borough, how chosen, 18

METROPOLIS,
    valuation in, 67
    rates levied in, 83
    expenditure in, 91

OVERSEERS,
    appointment and duties of, 3, 5, 24
    parish property vested in, 4
    assistant, appointment of, 3
    offices for, 4

OWNERS,
    voting of, 9, 22, 23, 100
    rating of, 27, 28, 102

PARISH,
    meaning of, 1, 5, 6
    history of, as unit of local government, 5
    assembly. See *Vestry*.
    officers, 3, 42, 110
    organization, purposes of, 4, 7
    rate, 4. See *Poor Rate*.
    property, 4, 5
    ecclesiastical, 1, 6
    poor-law, formation of, 5, 6
    highway, 38
    when a school district, 53
    meaning of, in Burial Acts, 58
    valuation of, 64, 66
    audit of accounts of, 66, 67
    considered as a primary area, 95
    adoption of Baths and Libraries Acts in, 109
    assessment of land-tax on, 115

PARISHES,
    number and boundaries of, 2, 6

PARLIAMENTARY PAPERS
    and debates, index of, 117

PAWNBROKERS,
    licensing of, 49

PEDLARS,
    licensing of, 49

PETROLEUM,
    licensing for, 48

PETTY SESSIONS. See *Justices*.

POLICE
    in counties and boroughs, 42, 43
    under local Acts, 44, 45
    metropolitan, 44
    number of forces of, 46

POLICE MAGISTRATE
    in a borough, 18
    in an urban district, 22

POOR-LAW,
    principles of, 24
    school districts, 54

POOR RELIEF,
    how given, 24, 25
    expenditure for, 26, 27, 89

POOR RATE,
    how raised, 4, 26, 27
    enforced by guardians, 10
    when paid by owners, 27, 28
    exemptions from, 28
    assessment of, 26, 64
    valuation for, conclusive for other rates, 64
    appeals against, 66
    recent increase in, 75, 83
    amount of expenditure from, 89, 90

PORT SANITARY AUTHORITIES,
    constitution and districts of, 31
    number of, 33

PRISONS,
    transfer to Government of, 81, 106
    visiting justices of, 107

PRIVY COUNCIL,
    control of, in respect of contagious diseases, 108

PUBLIC HEALTH ACT,
    See *Sanitary Purposes.*

PUBLIC WORKS LOANS COMMISSIONERS,
    powers of, 70, 113
    amount of loans advanced by, 72

QUARTER SESSIONS,
    in a county, 13
    in a borough, 18, 20
    highway powers of, 38
    the police authority, 43
    licensing at, 47, 48, 51
    powers of, in respect of reformatories, 54
    appeals to, against poor rates, 66
    appointment of inspectors and analyst by, 107
    appointment of conservators by, 114

RATE,
    See *Poor Rate, County Rate, Borough Rate, General District Rate.*
    when limited in amount, 7, 35, 36, 109, 112
    proposal to levy a consolidated, 102

RATEABLE VALUE,
    assessment of, 64
    recent increase in, 75, 80, 82
    compared with rates, 84

RECORDER,
    appointment of, 18
    without quarter sessions, 20

RECTOR,
    civil duties of, 3

REFORMATORIES
    and industrial schools, 54

REGISTRAR GENERAL,
    powers of, 108

REGISTRATION,
    of births and deaths, 10, 108
    of marriages and burials, 3

RIVERS,
    police on, 45
    embankment of, by Sewers Commissions, 61
    pollution of, 114
    may be formed into fishery districts, 114

ROADS,
    See *Main Roads, Highways.*

ROAD AUTHORITY,
    under Tramways Acts, 111

RURAL RATES,
    increase in, 76, 83
    expenditure from, 89, 90

RURAL SANITARY AUTHORITIES,
    constitution and powers of, 30, 32,
    when highway authorities, 36
    miscellaneous powers of, 113, 114

RURAL SANITARY DISTRICTS,
    number and boundaries of, 31
    when different from unions, 29, 32
    rate and expenditure in, 30, 32, 90

SANITARY PURPOSES,
    what are, 29, 114
    authorities for, 22, 29, 32

SANITARY RATE,
    See *General District Rate.*

SCHOOL ATTENDANCE COMMITTEE,
: appointment and powers of, 53, 54

SCHOOL BOARDS,
: election and duties of, 53
: numbers of, 55
: amount of debt of, 76, 83
: expenditure of, 90

SCHOOLS,
: See *Poor Law, Reformatories.*

SECRETARY OF STATE,
: control of police by, 43
: control of lunatic asylums by, 51
: powers in respect to burials of, 57
: appointment of prison commissioners by, 106
: appointment of factory inspectors by, 113
: power of, to form fishery districts, 114

SESSIONS,
: various kinds of, 13
:: See *Quarter Sessions, Justices.*

SETTLEMENT,
: poor-law, how acquired, 25

SEWERS,
: commissioners of, 61, 62
: under Public Health Act, 29, 63
: proposed system of special charges for, 103

SHERIFF,
: of a county, 13
: of a town, 20

SPECIAL DRAINAGE DISTRICT,
: what is a, 30

SLAUGHTER HOUSES,
: licenses for, 48

SURVEYOR
: of highways, 34

TAXES,
: commissioners for assessing, 115

THEATRES,
: licenses for, 48

TOWN COUNCIL,
: election and functions of, 17, 18
: powers over reformatories of, 54
:: See *Boroughs.*

TOWNS,
> counties of, 20

TOWNSHIP,
> how different from parish, 5, 38

TRAMWAY,
> construction of, by local authority, 111

TREASURY,
> powers of, in respect of local loans, 71
> subventions to local rates, amount of, 78, 80
> > analysis of, 92

TURNPIKES,
> lapse of, into highways, 37
> cost of maintenance of, 40
> in South Wales, 40

UNION CHARGEABILITY ACT,
> effect of, 10, 26
> doubtful justice of, 98

UNIONS,
> formation and alteration of, 8
> under local Acts, 11
> number and boundaries of, 11, 95, 97
> common fund of, 10, 26, 27, 108, 109
> settlement in, 25
> when rural sanitary districts, 29
> audit of accounts of, 66
> adoption of, as primary areas, 96
> alteration of, in urban districts, 98
> appointment of registrars and vaccinators in, 109

URBAN EXPENDITURE
> cannot be distinguished from rural, 73, 77
> amount and analysis of, 82, 86, 88

URBAN SANITARY DISTRICTS,
> what are, 21, 29
> number and boundaries of, 21, 31, 99
> how different from rural districts, 30
> highways in, 36, 39
> appointment of school attendance committees in, 54
> burial authority in, 57, 58
> adoption of Baths and Libraries Acts in, 109
> lighting in, 110
> artisans' dwellings, etc., in, 110—114

VALUATION,
> for county rate, 14
> under the Union Assessment Acts, 64—66
> ought to be simplified, 102

K

VESTRY,
    common and select, 2, 7
    chairman of, 2, 3
    rooms, 4
    powers of, 7, 109, 110
    provision of cemetery by, 56, 59

VESTRY CLERK,
    appointment and duties of, 3

WASHHOUSES,
    Acts relating to, 109

WATCHMEN,
    how appointed, 42

WATCH RATE,
    how levied, 18, 44

WATER SUPPLY,
    by sanitary authority, 29, 114
    expenditure on, 88, 90

WEIGHTS AND MEASURES,
    inspectors and standards of, 107

WORKHOUSE,
    relief in, 25

YARN,
    appointment of inspectors of, 107

THE END.

www.ingramcontent.com/pod-product-compliance
Lightning Source LLC
Chambersburg PA
CBHW030352170426
43202CB00010B/1345